A Rage for Glory

THE LIFE OF COMMODORE
STEPHEN DECATUR, USN

James Tertius de Kay

Free Press

NEW YORK LONDON TORONTO SYDNEY SINGAPORE

FREE PRESS

A Division of Simon & Schuster, Inc.

1230 Avenue of the Americas

New York, NY 10020

For information about special discounts for bulk purchases,
please contact Simon & Schuster Special Sales:
1-800-456-6798 or business@simonandschuster.com

Manufactured in the United States of America

1   3   5   7   9   10   8   6   4   2

Library of Congress Cataloging-in-Publication Data

De Kay, James T.
A rage for glory: the life of Commodore Stephen Decatur, USN/
James Tertius de Kay.
p.   cm.
Includes bibliographical references and index.
1. Decatur, Stephen, 1779–1820.   2. Admirals–United States–Biography.
3. United States. Navy–Biography.   4. United States–History–War of 1812–
Naval operations.   5. United States–History, Naval–To 1900.   I. Title.
E353.1.D29D15 2004
359'.0092–dc21
[B]
2003049248

ISBN 978-1-4165-6831-5

Again, for Bill Dunne

Contents

Contents

*The desire for glory clings even
to the best men longer than
any other passion.*

— TACITUS

A Rage for Glory

ONE

Washington City

The shocking news raced through Washington a little after ten o'clock on the morning of March 22, 1820. One of the first to hear of it was Secretary of State John Quincy Adams, who would record in his diary, "Before I left my house this morning to go to my office, W.S. Smith came in and told me Commodore Decatur had just been brought in from Bladensburg, mortally wounded in a duel."

The news came as a personal blow to Adams. Stephen Decatur, war hero and member of the Board of Navy Commissioners, was a neighbor and close friend. Only the night before, the commodore and his wife, Susan, had been guests at a grand party in the Adams home, given in honor of the marriage of President James Monroe's daughter.

Adams realized immediately that the tragedy was likely to have significant national repercussions. Decatur was a legendary figure throughout the young republic. His many spectacular acts of daring on the high seas were a source of national pride, and had won him every honor his country could bestow. More than simply the nation's reigning hero, he was an important political figure as well. Statesmen of every stripe sought him out for his opinions and support. At the age of forty-one he was recognized as a member of the new generation of leaders. There was talk that he might be destined for higher office, perhaps even the presidency.

After relaying the grim news to his wife, Louisa, Adams hurried across President's Square—the present Lafayette Park—to the Decatur residence. Anxious citizens were already gathering in front of the imposing town house that Decatur had built with prize money earned in his victorious naval actions. Pushing his way through the crowd Adams managed to gain the entrance. Smears of blood on the door jamb and along the corri-

1

dor walls inside showed where, only minutes before, the wounded man had been carried through to the reception room on the ground floor.

The house was already filling with high government officials, most of them well known to Adams. He was able to make his way through the throng to where he could catch a glimpse of the fallen commodore, sprawled awkwardly on a couch, surrounded by anxious retainers. It was an unnerving sight. Doctors, naval officers, and servants moved about anxiously, or huddled in corners, conversing in whispers. Decatur himself was almost unrecognizable. His face was ashen, his familiar features tortured into a rictal grimace as he struggled to deal with the pain. His bright piercing eyes, normally his most notable feature, were dull and listless. His high forehead and long, aquiline nose were smeared with dirt and scratches from the dueling field. The boyish forelock of wavy brown hair that the portraitists so delighted in lay matted and disheveled.

The pistol ball had glanced off his hip bone into the groin, severing vital arteries. The doctors had tried to stanch the flow of blood, but there was no place to apply a tourniquet, and they had been only partially successful. Wads of bloody makeshift bandages—towels, bedsheets, table linen—lay about, attesting to their frantic efforts.

Dr. Lowell, the U.S. surgeon-general, who had hurried over to assist the physicians already in attendance, made an optimistic pronouncement concerning Decatur's condition but Adams suspected his diagnosis was more to comfort family members than anything else. An army colonel who had managed to see Decatur at close hand told Adams that the wounded man could not survive the day.

Decatur's distress was obviously extreme. He knew he was a dying man and seemed almost to welcome the prospect. At one point he told the doctors he had not believed it was possible to endure such pain. The surgeons suggested probing the wound to extract the ball, but when Decatur asked whether such a step would ease the discomfort they admitted it would make no difference, so he told them to leave the bullet where it was. It had already done all the injury it could, he said.

The news of the fallen leader spread rapidly across town. The city of Washington was still little more than an overgrown village made up of flimsy rooming houses sandwiched between grandiose half-finished marble public palaces. On muddy street corners and in the halls of power citizens and officeholders gathered together to speak in hushed tones of the distressing event.

What had brought on such a terrible and unexpected catastrophe? It would be months, even years, before all the details of the duel became known, but even in the first hours after the tragedy the broad outlines of the story had already emerged. The duel had taken place at nine o'clock that morning just across the District line in Maryland at a place called the Valley of Chance in the village of Bladensburg. Decatur had come there in response to a challenge from Commodore James Barron, another naval officer, who had also been wounded in the encounter, but was expected to recover.

Details of the quarrel between the two men were still sketchy, but it was thought to have had its origin in an 1808 court-martial of Barron in which Decatur had sat as one of the judges. The court had convicted Barron and in the twelve years since the two men had neither met nor spoken until that very morning on the dueling grounds.

Twelve years! How could such a feud fester for so long? There was speculation that the quarrel might have been deliberately kept alive and encouraged by others. But for what dark reasons? Suspicions quickly fell on the duelists' two seconds, who were also high-ranking naval officers, Commodore William Bainbridge and Captain Jesse Duncan Elliott. Both men had already fled the city for the safety of Virginia, and there were rumors—which later proved unfounded—that the Navy Department had ordered the arrest of both men.

Decatur's fellow officers, the men who knew him best, asked different questions. How, they asked, could a man of such celebrated principle and such unquestioned courage allow himself to be drawn into such a tawdry and futile encounter? Decatur was no hot-blooded adolescent, anxious to prove his manhood. He was a mature leader, the bravest of the brave, and the man, incidentally, who had done more than any other to curb the practice of dueling in the navy. What had induced him to accept Barron's pitiful, trumped-up challenge, to throw away his life so cheaply? To many of those who knew him best, Decatur's death was worse than tragic, it was pointless.

By midafternoon, as it became increasingly clear that Decatur would not survive the day, President Monroe canceled a reception that had been planned for the evening, and he and the entire city, united in grief, mounted a mournful death watch.

Decatur finally died a little after ten o'clock that evening. The following day, Thursday, the *National Intelligencer* thundered: "A hero has fallen! Commodore Stephen Decatur . . . the pride of his country—the gallant and noble hearted gentleman—is no more!" Gushing on in the high-flown rhetoric of the day, the paper exhorted, "Mourn, Columbia! for one of our brightest stars is set—a son 'without fear and without reproach'—in the freshness of his fame—in the prime of his usefulness—has descended into the tomb. . . . He was amongst the first of those who have added to the fame of his country; and his premature death is mourned as it ought to be."

On Friday, the day of the funeral, government offices and most businesses in Washington were closed. In the House of Representatives John Randolph of Roanoke, one of the commodore's most fervent supporters, rose to move "that the speaker, officers and members of this House, attend the funeral of the late Stephen Decatur, Esquire, of the United States navy, from his late residence, at four o'clock this afternoon." Not every member concurred. The practice of dueling was generally tolerated, particularly among officers in the armed forces, but it was unequivocally against the law, and before Randolph's motion could be put to a vote a Mr. Holmes rose to oppose it, proposing that rather than submitting such a delicate matter to yeas and nays, he would move that the House simply adjourn, thus giving every gentleman an opportunity of indulging his own inclinations on this solemn and melancholy occasion. The motion was carried without dissent.

Long before the hour appointed for the funeral procession to begin, it became evident that the crowds of citizens who had come to pay their last respects to the fallen hero would far surpass any such demonstration previously seen in Washington. Since early morning people had been arriving individually and in small groups, sometimes in entire families, in wagons, carriages, on horseback, and on foot from the surrounding farms and suburbs. Stephen Decatur, who had never run for elective office, had clearly touched the lives of a multitude.

As the time approached to bring out the casket and escort it to its final resting place, some ten thousand mourners—in a city of barely fifteen thousand souls—had assembled in front of the Decatur residence and crowded into the surrounding streets, creating lines of humanity that stretched past the Executive Mansion—it was not yet known as the White House—and down Pennsylvania Avenue almost as far as the unfinished Capitol.

From the Washington Navy Yard in the southwest corner of the city came the regularly repeated boom of minute guns, solemnly marking the occasion. Soon, by prearrangement, the salutes of the cannon were joined by the tolling bells of every church in the District.

It was only with difficulty that the dignitaries and military honor guards managed to take their assigned places. When at last all was ready the procession started off, marching to muffled drums and funeral music, led by an honor guard of marines and followed by officers and men of the

United States Navy and Marine Corps, wearing crepe on the left sleeve in respect for the memory of the deceased. The coffin, borne by officers of the army and navy as pallbearers, was preceded by the clergy and followed by the distraught widow and other relatives. Next, by himself, marched President James Monroe, leading his entire cabinet, and followed by virtually every member of the Senate and the House of Representatives. After them came Chief Justice John Marshall and his associate judges. The entire tripartite leadership of the new republic—executive, legislative, and judicial—marched in silent tribute. They were followed by lesser officials of the federal government, officers of the District of Columbia, and the diplomatic corps. Last, shoulder to shoulder, came the thousands upon thousands of private citizens, in a crowd that stretched for almost half a mile. Never before had there been such an overwhelming demonstration of communal sorrow in the country's short history. Its equal would not be seen for another two generations, when a grieving public turned out to mourn Abraham Lincoln.

There was to be no formal church service. Although nominally an Episcopalian, Decatur had been a perfunctory churchgoer at best, and his widow had ruled out any elaborate religious ceremony as inappropriate. The procession made its way northwest to Kalorama, the grand estate owned by Decatur's closest friend, Colonel Bomford of the Ordnance Corps. It was in the burial vault of the estate that he was to be laid to rest. The mansion, with its magnificent view of Georgetown and the Potomac beyond (Kalorama was Greek for "beautiful vista"), stood near the present intersection of Rock Creek and Massachusetts Avenue. On arrival at the burial site, John Quincy Adams recorded, "A very short prayer was made at the vault by Dr. Hunter, and a volley of musketry from a detachment of the Marine Corps closed the ceremony over the earthly remains of a spirit as kindly, as generous, and as dauntless as breathed in this nation or on this earth."

On the other side of the empty city, in one of the upper rooms at Beale's Hotel, not far from Capitol Hill, a lone figure lay on a bed listening to the solemn, monotonous booming of the minute guns mixed with the doleful chorus of tolling church bells. He was Commodore James Barron, the man who fired the fatal shot that had brought Decatur down, and who was recuperating from the wound he had received at Bladensburg. From the doctor who ministered to him he learned of the huge crowds and the almost endless procession of mourners.

After what seemed a very long time the minute guns finally fell silent, the bells stopped tolling, and the world outside his window grew still, signaling that the ceremonies had come to an end. In the silence of his hotel room James Barron was left to ponder his responsibility for bringing forth such an upwelling of public grief and to assess his own future, which would inevitably be shaped by it. No matter what fate might hold for him in the years to come, he knew that he now bore the mark of Cain, and would forever more be remembered simply as the man who killed Stephen Decatur.

In an age before the electric telegraph or steam railways, when even the most momentous news could travel only at the speed that a horse or sailing vessel might carry it, the mournful tidings of Decatur's death spread slowly across the land. The citizens of Boston to the north, and Charleston to the south, were only just learning the first shocking accounts of the duel on the day of the funeral, and it would be weeks before the more remote areas of the country heard the news.

Wherever and whenever the news arrived, the people gathered in sorrow. Yellowing newspaper accounts of public mourning, official proclamations of grief, and some truly awful funereal poems ("Decatur falls! Another victim Honor's Moloch claims!") attest to the depth of loss his fellow citizens attached to his passing. There was something in his character, something in the sheer audacity of his achievements, that touched them profoundly. To perpetuate his memory, they named their streets, their parks, their municipalities in his honor. The numerous towns and cities scattered over at least a dozen states that still bear his name attest to the fact that Stephen Decatur—brave, noble Decatur—was a man his countrymen wanted very much to remember.

TWO

Philadelphia

S tephen Decatur was born on January 5, 1779. The date is not without significance. It lies at the midpoint of the American Revolution, a little more than two years after the signing of the Declaration of Independence and another two years before Washington's triumph at Yorktown that brought the war to an end. The Revolution and its aftermath would influence every aspect of his life. If he grew up to be a hero, it was in part because he was born into an age of heroes, an age when Americans, having won their freedom from the world's most powerful empire, were convinced they could accomplish anything they set their mind to. It was a time of unusual opportunity and breathtaking achievement, a time when John Adams of Massachusetts could write Richard Henry Lee of Virginia, "You and I, my dear friend, have been sent into life at a time when the greatest lawgivers of antiquity would have wished to live. How few of the human race have ever enjoyed [such] an opportunity . . . for themselves or their children."

Appropriately for a future American hero, Decatur was born in a simple wooden cabin, in the tiny hamlet of Sinepuxent, on Maryland's eastern shore, where his family had fled to escape from the British occupation of their native Philadelphia.

The Decaturs had good reason to hide from the British. Stephen's father, also named Stephen, was master of a privateer and spent much of the war at sea, hunting down English merchant vessels under a letter of marque and reprisal issued by the Continental Congress. The obscure hamlet of Sinepuxent, conveniently located between Chesapeake Bay and the open Atlantic and accessible from both, allowed the elder Stephen to visit his little family, consisting of his wife, Ann, their young daughter, also named Ann, and now their infant Stephen, Jr., between cruises.

Later that year, after General Howe had moved his redcoats back into the field, the Decaturs were able to return to their home in Philadelphia, where young Stephen would grow up.

Philadelphia in the closing decades of the eighteenth century would have been a particularly stimulating place in which to live, and undoubtedly it helped shape the young Decatur's character and worldview. It was a city of great commercial dynamism and cultural sophistication. It was the largest city in America, bigger and more important than either New York or Boston, a thriving metropolis of some thirty thousand people living in austere but elegant brick homes on well-cobbled, tree-lined streets. The city, situated about a hundred miles up the Delaware River at its junction with the Schuylkill, was a major center of trade, with extensive commercial and cultural ties throughout the United States and overseas. Along the waterfront, ships laden with agricultural produce from the outlying farms of Pennsylvania, New Jersey, and Delaware competed for space with merchantmen newly returned from Europe and the West Indies with cargoes of manufactured goods, sugar, and rum.

Culturally, the city was presided over by the worldly spirit of Benjamin Franklin, patriot, statesman, and resident genius, and could boast an unequaled array of newspapers (including America's first daily), excellent schools, and a number of well-regarded learned societies.

Philadelphia, during most of the years of Decatur's childhood and youth, was also the capital of the United States, and as such was a lively laboratory of passionate debate and political experimentation. It was dominated by military leaders and statesmen who had risked their lives and fortunes in the name of liberty, and won. They carried within themselves a heightened sense of national destiny, and were eagerly creating a radically new kind of nation.

The youthful Stephen Decatur, who would grow up accustomed to the sight of such legendary leaders as George Washington, Alexander Hamilton, and James Madison walking the streets of his neighborhood, would consciously model himself upon them. His entire life would reflect the optimism, the willingness to risk, the occasional hubris, and the tendency to overreach that characterized his country in those first formative years of its existence.

Unlike most of their neighbors in Philadelphia, who were of predominantly English stock, the Decatur family included Dutch, French, Scottish, and Irish bloodlines, and traced its roots to the Netherlands, where early in the seventeenth century a De Kater ancestor left Amsterdam for Bordeaux and married a French woman "of noble rank." In the late 1740s a descendant of this union, a young French naval officer named Etienne Decatur, turned up in Newport, Rhode Island, where he married a local girl, Priscilla Hill. The young couple produced a son, born in 1751 and named Stephen, after his father.

Etienne had difficulty finding work in Newport, and later that year the Decaturs moved to Philadelphia. Etienne hoped to find work there as a merchant captain, but he died soon after his arrival in one of the yellow fever epidemics that periodically plagued the city. The young widow was left penniless with a new baby in a strange town. Somehow she managed to raise her son, and when he was of age he left home to follow the family profession of the sea, having learned at first hand from his mother invaluable lessons on the importance of perseverance and determination. They were lessons that would flower in spectacular fashion in Priscilla's grandson.

With the Revolution won, the senior Decatur, who had amassed a considerable fortune from his activities as a privateer, entered into partnership with the Philadelphia firm of Gurney & Smith, waterfront merchants and ship owners. In his capacity as a ship's captain he made regular voyages to Bordeaux in the company's vessels. His duties necessarily kept him away from home for long periods, but despite his frequent absences he exer-

cised a strong influence on his son. The young Stephen Decatur, Jr., grew
up in comfortable circumstances. He would later remember the romantic
mystique associated with his father, the excitement that filled the house
every time he returned, and the warmth of those evenings when the entire
family, grown larger over the years by the addition of two younger brothers, James and John, sat mesmerized by his father's colorful tales of adventures and faraway places. He would remember too how all the excitement
associated with his father's presence would quickly dissipate when he
sailed off again, and life reverted once more to familiar routine. Decatur's
earliest exposure to formal education was under the tutelage of a widowed
neighbor, a Mrs. Gordon, whose husband had been lost at sea, and who
taught him and his sister the basics of spelling and sums. Mrs. Gordon's
influence on the little boy must have been considerable, for he maintained
a lifelong devotion to her, and continued to provide support for her in her
old age.

A formative event—almost certainly the most important one in
Stephen's life—occurred during the summer of 1787, when he was eight
years old. Over the winter, he had suffered from a severe bout of whoop-
ing cough, and by springtime was still having difficulties recovering. It was
decided that a good dose of sea air might help, so his father took him as a
passenger on his next voyage to France, on board his ship *Ariel*. For a
bright and perceptive boy who worshiped his father and was curious
about the world, such an adventure would have been an unforgettable
experience.

Poets from before the time of Homer have sought to describe the mys-
teries and enchantment of the sea, but to the young Decatur no poetry
would have been necessary. Watching the familiar sights of the Philadelphia waterfront fall away as the ship made her way down the Delaware to
Chester and the sea, seeing the wind catch her sails, and watching them
fill out into a cloud of canvas above his head, pushing the ship beyond the
sight of land, was to enter a world little short of magical.

The novelty and excitement of that summer would stay with him for a
lifetime . . . the evocative smells of pitch and pine, the sting of salt air, the

bewildering cat's cradle of ropes that soared overhead, the mysterious language of larboard and starboard, of belaying pins and turk's heads, of deadeyes and shrouds, messengers and halyards . . . all such strange and unfamiliar things might have been a heady and confusing mystery, were not their names and functions patiently explained to him by his father, that demigod in charge of a world of wonders, that Prospero whose wisdom and skill guided the *Ariel* on her way.

The arrival in the Gironde, and the voyage upriver to their destination at Bordeaux, must have been more exciting still. To step upon an unfamiliar shore, and walk down strange streets in a city where everyone spoke a foreign tongue, would have engendered permanent memories. At the tender age of eight, Stephen Decatur was experiencing what most of his generation would never know at first hand—the knowledge that a wholly different world lay out there beyond the horizon, waiting to be discovered and challenged.

Undoubtedly the most important impression Stephen brought back from that memorable voyage was the image of his father on the quarterdeck: his father determining the ship's course, giving orders that were obeyed without question, accepting the deference of his inferiors, secure in the knowledge of his own palpable worthiness. Here, right before his eyes, was the ultimate metaphor of the man in charge: the captain of the ship, master of all he surveyed. Could any young boy not be deeply influenced by such an image?

On Stephen's return, his parents decided it was time to enroll him in a more formal educational facility. His mother, a devout Episcopalian, harbored hopes that he might some day enter the ministry, and with that in mind entered him at the nearby Episcopal Academy on Fourth Street, where he would study under the direction of a local rector, the Reverend Dr. James Abercrombie. The Academy was one of the leading schools in Philadelphia, and among his fellow students were three boys who were destined to play significant roles in Stephen's adult life—Charles Stewart and Richard Somers, future naval officers, and Richard Rush, who would grow up to become a statesman and member of the presidential cabinet.

At his new school Decatur quickly established a reputation for enthusiasm and intellectual curiosity that was coupled, alas, with indifferent scholarship. While he was obviously bright and articulate, his marks rarely reflected his intelligence. Despite all of Dr. Abercrombie's efforts, he was simply not a good student. Apparently, under Mrs. Gordon's gentle attentions he learned well enough, but he did not fare as well under the more formal strictures of a traditional classroom environment.

The Decatur home was on Front Street near the Philadelphia docks, and inevitably the Delaware River became a favorite haunt of the young Stephen. He was a resourceful youth who enjoyed fishing and was handy with boats, and he could always find something to occupy his time. Many years after his death his schoolmate and friend Richard Rush remembered an incident that occurred during those childhood years. "We used to bathe in the Delaware, near a bank called 'the old fort,' in the neighborhood where the navy yard now is. Once, while the boys were swimming about, a few made for a ship moored to a wharf at hand, that they might dive from her side. One of them ran up the bowsprit quite out to the tip end of the jib-boom, from which he instantly plunged head foremost into the stream. It was Decatur. Shouts rose from the boys, and the very sailors may have been amazed, as the ship was large, and the height seemed fearful."

Clearly, the young Decatur exhibited at an early age what a later generation would call "the right stuff." It is worth noting in passing that swimming was not a common skill in those days, and that most of the officers and men with whom Decatur would sail over the years could not swim a stroke.

Because Philadelphia was a major seaport as well as the national capital, the city was always highly sensitive to shifts and changes in the outside world. When Britain and France went to war in 1793, many called for America to take sides in the conflict, but President Washington was determined to keep out of it altogether, and despite provocations from both powers he was largely successful in steering clear of any involvement. But while he managed to keep his country out of the European war, other foreign entanglements proved to be more difficult to avoid. Particularly troublesome were the problems created by the Barbary pirates of North Africa. The four Barbary states—Morocco, Algiers, Tunis, and Tripoli—had for centuries been operating what amounted to a seaborne protection racket in the Mediterranean. Their strategy was simple. They sent out swift, heavily armed corsairs to prey on merchant ships, and whenever they captured one they would enslave her crew, and then demand a ransom for the return of the ship and the men. The simplest way for a country to protect its ships against capture was to agree to pay an annual tribute to the pirates. Even mighty Great Britain, with its world-girdling navy, felt constrained to pay such tribute.

The American government was reluctant to adopt the practice of buying off the Barbary predators, but since the country had no navy with which to protect its merchant ships it had no alternative, so long as it wished to trade in the Mediterranean. America's total lack of sea power was deliberate, and reflected national policy. Most members of Congress did not want a navy because they feared that an armed fleet would inevitably lead the country into dangerous mischief overseas. They argued that while it might be humiliating and expensive to pay off the Barbary pirates, at least it avoided war.

The fallacy of this position became evident when one of the Barbary states, Algiers, decided unilaterally to abrogate its treaty with the American government and demanded more money. While the dey of Algiers awaited an American response, he reverted to the practice of capturing any American vessel his corsairs came across and enslaving her crew.

An aroused Congress finally decided to overcome its distaste for warships and resolved "that a naval force, adequate to the protection of the commerce of the United States against the Algerine corsairs, ought to be provided." The Naval Act of March 1794 marks the birth of the United States Navy, and authorized the president "to provide, by purchase or otherwise, equip and employ, four ships to carry forty-four guns and two ships to carry thirty-six guns each." The act limited the navy to only these six ships, a laughably small sea force by world standards, but it was hoped that this modest fleet would be enough to buy a little respect from the Barbary pirates. The sum of $688,888.82 was appropriated to begin construction.

As with almost every military appropriation from that day to this, Congress made sure to spread the money over as many states as possible. Each ship was to be built in a different seaport. One of the first contracts was let to Gurney & Smith, the Philadelphia naval agents with which Stephen Decatur, Sr. was affiliated. The company was selected to build one of the big forty-four-gun ships, identified at that point simply as Frigate B.

It was around this time that Stephen Decatur's formal education came to an abrupt end. He had left the Episcopal Academy and was enrolled at the grammar school of the College of Pennsylvania, but if his parents had hoped that the change might improve his academics, they were doomed to disappointment. Their eldest son, for all his energy and intelligence, was simply not a scholar. At the age of fifteen or perhaps sixteen at the latest, he dropped out of school, never to return. It was obvious that with his weak academics he never could fulfill his mother's dream of the ministry, but the deciding factor leading to the end of his academic career may well have been Gurney & Smith's contract to build Frigate B. He was already looking forward to a life somehow connected to the sea, and the prospect that a major warship would be constructed so close to his home, under the supervision of a company with which his father maintained close ties, may well have presented an opportunity too good to pass up. In any case, soon after he abandoned his education he was hired by Gurney & Smith.

The new forty-four-gun American frigates authorized by Congress had all been designed by Joshua Humphreys, one of the young republic's leading naval architects, who had put aside his pacifist Quaker principles to create what were to become the most technically advanced warships of the age.

"If we build our ships the same size as the Europeans, they having so great a number of them, we shall always be behind them," he argued. "I would build them of a larger size than theirs, and take the lead to them, which is the only safe method of commencing a navy."

For the next eighteen months Stephen Decatur, working full-time at Gurney & Smith, had the opportunity to witness on a daily basis the construction of an entirely new class of warship, one that would in time be recognized the world over for its innovative design and impressive fighting qualities. She would have the largest spars, the greatest spread of canvas, the thickest sides, and the heaviest batteries of any frigate then afloat, and she would realize her designer's dream of a frigate that "should combine such qualities of strength, durability, swiftness of sailing, and force, as to render her superior to any frigate belonging to the European Powers."

Joshua Humphreys was at the shipyard every day, making sure his workmen followed his plans precisely. So too was the frigate's designated captain, Commodore John Barry, a veteran of the Revolution who had fought in the old Continental Navy and was the man George Washington had personally selected to be the ranking officer of the new navy. As often as not, President Washington himself, an eloquent proponent of a strong navy, would take time from his executive duties to come down and inspect the ship.

Less noticed than such luminaries, but always present, was the young Decatur, taking note of each day's progress, absorbing at first hand an intimate knowledge of a warship that, as the fates would have it, he would one day take into battle. Stephen Decatur, the indifferent scholar, had no trouble understanding Humphreys's plans or grasping the elegant logic of his design.

By the time she was ready for launching, Frigate B had received her proper name: the USS *United States*. On July 10, 1797, with flags flying, bugles blaring, cannon roaring, and with an immense crowd of nearly twenty thousand cheering onlookers in attendance, workmen began to cut away the blocks that had held the frigate in place for a year and a half, and slowly and majestically the vessel slid gracefully and almost silently down the greased ways and into the Delaware. Standing on the spar deck along with a multitude of others, Stephen Decatur would have savored the moment.

At the age of nineteen it was time for Decatur to decide upon a career. The choice must have seemed self-evident. The nascent U.S. Navy was looking for a number of young men to become midshipmen, to be trained into officers to command the future fleet. Secretary of the Navy Benjamin Stoddert had a very clear idea of the kind of candidates he wanted. He was looking for "sprightly young men of good education, good character, and good connections." Ideally, the service was looking for lads of fifteen or sixteen. The prevailing wisdom held that beyond the age of eighteen a young man's character was likely to be too deeply rooted to be trained and molded into that of a proper naval officer. Decatur was already a little long in the tooth to be an ideal candidate, and his educational credentials were less than stellar, but he was otherwise eminently qualified. The fact that his father was a respected veteran of the War of Independence, and that he was also a personal friend and old comrade of Commodore Barry, stood very much in his favor.

Barry enthusiastically endorsed the young man's candidacy, and promised to use his influence to obtain a place for him. But a midshipman's warrant was not all that easy to obtain, even for someone as well placed as Barry. A naval career was looked upon as a gentlemanly and honorable profession, and many a senator's son was already on the waiting list. Possibly to improve the young Decatur's chances, his father engaged a former Royal Navy officer, Talbot Hamilton, to tutor his son in navigation and other nautical sciences.

But Decatur need not have worried. In due course his warrant arrived, dated April 30, 1798, and signed by Secretary Stoddert and President John Adams. The next morning, the young man stepped on board the *United States* and reported for duty. He and the navy had found each other.

THREE

Mr. Midshipman Decatur

At the age of nineteen, Stephen Decatur had reached his full growth. He was now a rugged, well-filled-out young man, standing just short of six feet, and very much aware that he cut a dashing figure in his brand new midshipman's uniform, which was only marginally less glamorous than that of a commissioned officer. His prominent nose, high forehead, and wavy, dark brown hair highlighted his almost Latinate features, and his large, dark eyes suggested a quick mind and a sharply honed sense of curiosity.

Secretary Stoddert might almost have had him in mind when he set out the qualities he was looking for in midshipmen. "A spirit of enterprise and adventure cannot be too much encouraged," he wrote, and in an observation that neatly combined idealism with a certain worldly wisdom, "Bravery is a quality not to be dispensed with in the officers. Like charity, it covers a great many defects." Stoddert recognized that the American navy would perforce be small, and its officers would have to make up for that deficiency. "If our officers cannot be inspired by the true kind of zeal and spirit which will enable us to make up for the want of great force by great activity, we had better burn our ships and commence a navy at some future time when our citizens have more spirit."

A midshipman's salary was nineteen dollars a month. It was a fairly liberal wage by the standards of the day, given the fact that it included room and board, and compares not unfavorably with Commodore Barry's compensation, which came to $117 a month. Naval officers were expected to supplement their income with prize money. Given the disproportionate way prize money was divided, with senior officers getting the lion's share, Barry could with any luck expect to augment his meager earnings considerably, should his squadron manage to catch sufficient enemy vessels. The lowly midshipmen, and the even more lowly sailors, far down on the list of preferments, could expect little more than pocket change.

Shipboard life, with its special rules, complex duties, and arcane language, could be an intimidating world for the uninitiated, but Decatur adapted easily to it. He was already thoroughly familiar with the ship, having observed her construction at first hand, and he already knew important members of the ship's company. The captain, of course, was a family friend, but he was also pleased to find that two boyhood companions had already preceded him on board. Charles Stewart, who had dropped out of school at an even earlier age than Decatur and had subsequently gone to sea, had been appointed fourth lieutenant of the *United States* on the basis of his years in the merchant service. Richard Somers, another schoolmate from the Episcopal Academy, was a fellow midshipman.

There was much for the midshipmen to learn, and the rudiments of seamanship and sailing were only part of their education. Their basic responsibility was to help the commissioned officers, and by so doing learn to become one. There is a story of Decatur's tour as a midshipman that he often told on himself. Everything on board a sailing ship has a specific name, and if an officer wished to refer to "the main topmast preventer stay," it was imperative that he call it by that name and no other. But Decatur had trouble remembering the names and purposes of the various ropes that controlled the sails and yards. To overcome his difficulty, he secretly wrote the names in pencil behind the belaying rails where the lines were secured. His system worked well enough during the daylight hours, but how he managed at night, with only starlight to help him decipher his notes, he neglected to explain.

The ship's company totaled approximately four hundred officers and men, and was divided into two watches, the starboard watch under the supervision of the first and third lieutenants, and the larboard watch under the second and fourth lieutenants. Decatur was assigned to the starboard watch, and as a result came into close and regular contact with a man who was destined to play a unique role in his navy career. He was James Barron, third lieutenant of the *United States,* and the man who would, years later, kill him on the dueling grounds of Bladensburg.

Barron was a tall man, well over six feet, with a deep chest and broad shoulders, tested and strengthened by years of strenuous life at sea. He had a round, pleasing face, with an open countenance that bespoke a genial nature. He was ten years older than Decatur, and had already spent almost twenty years at sea, having enlisted in the Virginia navy at the age of eleven, and served under his father in the Revolution. After the war, he had gone directly into the merchant service.

The two men hit it off from the start, the older responding warmly to Decatur's obvious intelligence, drive, and eagerness to learn. Barron, a Virginian with the deeply felt sensitivity to personal honor characteristic of his class, was to have great influence on the emerging Decatur, and would serve as an important role model. His steady nature and highly competent technical skills quickly earned Decatur's respect, and in later years Decatur would freely admit that he had once revered Barron as his own father.

As events would prove, it was not a reverence that would stand the test of time.

By the summer of 1798, when the frigate was preparing to go to sea for the first time, her mission had changed significantly. She had been originally authorized by Congress specifically to do battle with the Algerine pirates, but that quarrel had long since been settled by diplomatic means, and Algiers and the other Barbary states were pacified, at least for the time being. But even with the North African corsairs momentarily quiescent, the revolutionary government of France emerged as a new threat to American freedom of the seas. The French were convinced that America was siding with Great Britain in the European war, and in consequence French warships and privateers were ordered to hunt down and capture American merchant vessels. By 1798 the French navy had already taken literally hundreds of Yankee merchantmen in prize. It was an undeclared war—or as it was termed, a Quasi-War—and despite vigorous protestations from the American government, France made no effort to curb the predations of its warships.

The United States government was reluctant to fight back against such a powerful enemy, but by the summer of 1798 French depredations could no longer be tolerated, and those members of the national government in favor of defending American interests were able to move Congress to authorize the navy to retaliate, and to start capturing French armed vessels wherever they could be found. Captain Barry's orders called for him to sail to the West Indies where French privateers had been particularly active. In the last hurried days before departure, Midshipman Stephen Decatur was treated to what must have been one of the most gratifying experiences in his young life.

In the middle of June, by which time Decatur had been on board a little over six weeks, the *United States* dropped down the Delaware to Chester, where she would take on her final provisions. At dawn on the morning of July 8, the USS *Delaware,* a twenty-gun armed merchantman commanded by Decatur's father, made her way triumphantly upriver toward Chester in company with the French privateer *La Croyable,* which she had just captured. As Decatur, Sr., using a speaking trumpet, related the tale of his victory to Captain Barry, it is easy to imagine the pride of his eldest son, standing among the officers and men crowding the side of their ship, cheering the first American prize of the Quasi-War.

Five days later, the *United States,* ready for sea at last, spread her 42,720 square feet of sail—virtually an acre of canvas—and cleared the Delaware Capes on her maiden voyage.

The prospect of a possible encounter with an enemy brought a new level of intensity to the midshipmen's training. They had already had some indoctrination in the exercise of the great guns while still in harbor, but once at sea the guns became the center of each day's activities. Guns were the sole justification for the ship's existence, the officers explained. The ship was in fact nothing more than a gun platform, and it was only when the guns were in range of the enemy that the purpose of the navy came into sharp focus: to protect American interests, either by waging war or by suggesting such a possibility.

The ship's main battery, the thirty twenty-four-pounder long guns arrayed on either side of the gun deck, were divided into three divisions, forward, midships, and after, each commanded by a lieutenant, assisted by one or two midshipmen. Each gun was in turn handled by its own crew of ten to twelve hands, led by a gun captain.

Every day, each crew was repeatedly put through the multiple-step drill of casting loose the guns, loading them, priming them, firing them, controlling their recoil with breaching ropes, worming and sponging them, and then reloading them before finally housing them properly so as to leave them bowsed up and secure, impervious to wave and weather, and ready at a moment's notice to be cast loose again.

There was special training for each member of the gun crew, from the powder monkeys—often boys as young as ten years old—who had to be taught the safest, fastest, and most efficient way to carry the felt cartridge bags from the magazine to the gun deck, to the gun captains, who needed to know how to manage every kind of emergency.

And emergencies there were bound to be, because the guns were monsters, eight feet long and weighing over two tons, and each one willful and temperamental as a thoroughbred. Once quickened with sufficient gunpowder to bring them to life—usually eight pounds of the stuff, or one-third the weight of a round of shot—they took on a will of their own. In calm seas, the recoil from a twenty-four-pounder could smash a man's limbs and leave him crippled for life. On a pitching deck in foul weather, they could kill and wound their own crews with the same efficiency with which they dispatched the enemy.

Life at sea fell quickly into a routine for the midshipmen, as every day, through either the repetition of familiar activities or the occasional application to instructional texts, they grew increasingly knowledgeable in the ways that defined the highly specialized world of naval officers. It was the desire of President John Adams that "there ought to be a school on board every frigate," and midshipmen were supposed to gain proficiency in or at least familiarity with mathematics and navigation, and of course gunnery, but possibly the most important learning experience came during their idle hours, when "the young gentlemen" as they were known, retired to their quarters in the steerage, just forward of the wardroom on the berth deck.

Midshipmen were officers, and while they only held warrants, signed by the president, rather than commissions, which required Senate confirmation as well, they were entitled to the privileges of their rank. Sequestered in their badly ventilated and ill-lighted quarters, they would eat, drink, sing bawdy songs, and generally carry on like young men of their age the world over, forming friendships and cliques, sometimes quarreling, and always exploring, in long, drawn-out discussions, the infinite aspects of their chosen career. What was the greatest form of valor? Which weapons were best for boarding? What were the most important qualifications for leadership? It was here that Decatur absorbed the core ideas underlying the naval ethos: the doctrine that victory at sea depended primarily on daring commanders, and the concept that personal honor, ship's honor, and national honor were all inextricably linked, and must be preserved at all costs.

The close examination of honor, and of its cognates, glory and fame, were an endless source of fascination for naval officers in general and midshipmen in particular. The three concepts formed a trinity of ideals that underlay the belief structure that was the foundation of the life they had chosen.

Fame, as it was perceived in the steerage of the frigate *United States,* was very different from our present-day understanding of the word, and would probably be closer in meaning to our "renown." Honor could be inherited, but fame had to be earned, and earned only by acts of such nobility and good character that the world, of its own accord, would be forced to pay heed and express its approbation.

Glory was the most difficult of the three concepts to define. Everyone could recognize it, but few could agree to its meaning, perhaps because glory was deeply rooted in Christian doctrine, and the midshipmen were not the least interested in its religious connotations. To them glory arose out of the ethic of competition, of combat, of struggle for eminence and distinction, of pride of place, all of which was antithetical to its Christian meaning of a gift through the grace of God.

To defend honor, to court fame for its own sake, and to seek glory wherever it might be found: It was these very worldly perceptions and values that would define Decatur's character and shape his life, much as they had already shaped the lives of the most revered Americans—preeminently George Washington, but virtually all the other Founders as well.

The first cruise of the *United States* lasted barely six weeks. It was perceived as something of a disappointment, since it resulted in only two captures, but Commodore Barry could take satisfaction from the fact that his squadron had served a valuable purpose by alerting the French privateers to the fact that they could no longer hunt down American shipping with impunity. As a result of the cruise, French activity against Yankee shipping decreased dramatically, and brought down with it the soaring insurance rates that American shippers had been forced to pay to cover their risks. It is estimated that in the course of the Quasi-War, the American navy saved shippers nearly nine million dollars in insurance costs by their active pursuit of French privateers. The entire cost of the navy from 1794 through 1798 had been only about two and a half million dollars, and the fact that a strong navy helped American business interests quickly became a fiscal argument that the navalists in Congress never tired of quoting, in their unceasing efforts to expand the fleet.

In September 1798 the *United States* left on a second cruise to the West Indies, one that would provide Decatur with his first experience of a major storm at sea and would occasion a heroic demonstration of seamanship that would be the making of the frigate's third lieutenant, James Barron.

On October 19, while off Cape Hatteras, the ship ran headlong into a violent gale. Raging winds created thirty-foot waves and great green seas repeatedly crashed over the deck, sweeping all before them. Day after day, the storm continued without letup. It was only by a miracle that no hands were lost. The ship, helpless to escape the fury of the wind, pitched and rolled on her beam ends. Commodore Barry was forced to let her scud before the wind, lurching along at ten knots, in the hope that she would ride it out.

The frigate had been partially recaulked and her rigging refitted following her maiden cruise, and now the warm winds of the Gulf Stream began softening the tar that reinforced the standing rigging, causing the shrouds and stays that held the masts in place to stretch and sag. The masts, no longer firmly anchored, began to shift in their steps, and to hammer at the keel like mighty pile drivers, threatening to smash the ship's most vital timbers.

The perilous situation was suddenly made infinitely more dangerous when a rogue wave cracked the bowsprit, further weakening the system of stays that held the huge masts in place. The ship seemed ready to founder.

It was at this dramatic moment that Lieutenant Barron volunteered to lead a team that would attempt to save the masts by fastening new lines, or purchases, to the slack rigging, drawing them taut, and securing them. It was a desperate undertaking, and Commodore Barry was at first reluctant to let Barron try, but finally gave his permission when it became clear there was no alternative. Moments later Barron and his men, all volunteers, began working their way slowly and methodically down the spar deck from foremast to main to mizzen, laboriously securing purchases to alternate shrouds, starboard and larboard, like lacing a boot. Drenched to the skin and in constant peril of being swept overboard with no possibility of rescue, they continued working for several hours, and eventually managed to stabilize the masts and thereby save the ship.

When the storm finally blew itself out after nine days, a crippled *United States* limped into Norfolk in need of a new bowsprit and a complete rerigging from stem to stern. If the crew showed a particular deference to the ship's third lieutenant, it was because every man, from the captain to the youngest boy, knew he almost certainly owed his life to James Barron.

Barry recommended Barron for promotion to captain, stating in his letter to the secretary of the navy that he was "as good an officer and as fit to command as any in the service, and I hope when you do promote him, you will give him a Ship that will enable him to do credit to himself and honor to his country." To Barry's great satisfaction, Barron was at once raised to the rank of captain, and Barry, who would continue to use the *United States* as his flagship, was able to appoint Barron his flag captain, and turn over command of the ship to him.

FOUR

Honor

The leaders of the new navy consciously sought to encourage a certain swagger in their midshipmen, a hauteur that it was hoped would instill in them a fighting spirit and turn callow youths into zealous leaders of men. By and large their efforts were successful, but sometimes, when those highly desirable characteristics were combined with the rigid perception of honor to which midshipmen attached such importance, they produced a volatile mix that on occasion led to the development of a breed of thin-skinned, high-spirited gamecocks ready to take umbrage at almost any blink, cough, or movement of an eyebrow that could possibly be interpreted as offensive.

With so many highly sensitive young men crowded into the confined quarters on board warships, it was inevitable that the practice of dueling would quickly become ingrained in naval life, so much so that in the years between 1798 and the Civil War, two-thirds as many American naval officers were to die in duels as in all of the country's sea fights. To be ready to die for your principles, or to kill a fellow officer in the defense of those same principles, became the bedrock of the naval ethos, and dueling was universally accepted and recognized as proof that you were not simply an officer, but a gentleman.

The standard authority on the fine points of dueling was the *code duello*, which came in various versions. The one generally followed in America had been codified by some Irish gentlemen in 1777. It listed all the generally approved terms of engagement and defined the etiquette involved in calling out an offender or accepting a challenge. Every midshipman knew the twenty-six articles of the code (sometimes known as the twenty-six commandments) by heart. But knowing the rules and deciding how to interpret them were quite different things, and the midshipmen's ideas of what constituted an act offensive enough to warrant a call to the field of honor could be, at times, little short of bizarre.

While still a midshipman Stephen Decatur was involved in an incident on board the *United States* that demonstrates just how far the *code duello* could be twisted and mangled by overly literal young minds. One day while the ship was in port between West Indian cruises, Decatur and Richard Somers were preparing to go on shore together. The two young men had been close since boyhood, and the strong bond they shared was often expressed in friendly banter. As they made their preparations, Somers, in the presence of the ship's other midshipmen, made a joking comment about Decatur's foppish dress. Decatur, responding in the same flippant spirit, accused Somers of playing the fool. The two continued chatting in the same vein until they left the gun room together and made their way up to the spar deck and their waiting boat. Neither young man was aware that their shipmates had taken their joking insults far more seriously than had ever been intended.

Down in the steerage the other midshipmen discussed the exchange between the two friends at great length. Eventually they decided that Decatur, by calling Somers a fool, had grossly insulted him, and that Somers, by taking no notice of Decatur's affront and continuing to remain on friendly terms with him, had demonstrated extreme cowardice and lack of honor.

A couple of days later, when Somers invited some of the other midshipmen to share a bottle of wine, he was taken aback when each one in turn stonily refused to drink with him. Puzzled and hurt, he demanded an explanation, and they told him of their solemn judgment of his earlier conversation with Decatur. They explained loftily that given Somers's craven cowardice, they could not consistent with their own honor take wine with him until the affair should be cleared up to their satisfaction, either by a formal apology on the part of Decatur, or by a call to the field. Somers was dumbfounded. He stormed out of the room and went in search of Decatur and told him what had happened. Decatur thought it was all very funny, and laughingly dismissed the matter as schoolboy posturing. But Somers was not amused. He had seen for himself how serious the other midshipmen were. After considerable soul-searching, he came to a fateful decision. He had been insulted, all right, but not by Decatur, but by all the other midshipmen. They had openly questioned his courage, and therefore his honor, and it was up to him to demand satisfaction. His only recourse, as he saw it, was to fight each one of them.

Decatur still refused to take the matter seriously. He thought Somers's judgment was as flawed as that of the other midshipmen and begged him to reconsider. He offered to give a dinner for the whole group, where he would not apologize, of course, but would publicly assure each of the offended young gentlemen that he had never entertained the most remote idea of offering an insult to Somers. But no argument could induce Somers to depart from the course he had chosen. He sat down and wrote out a challenge to each one of the midshipmen in turn, inviting them to meet him on the field of honor, each at a different hour on the same day. Decatur, serving reluctantly as his second, delivered the challenges, all of which were accepted.

On the appointed day the first midshipman showed up as scheduled, and in their duel Somers was hit by a ball in his right arm. When the second midshipman arrived, Decatur was concerned that because of his friend's wound, he would not be able to defend himself, and he offered to take his place. But Somers refused. Decatur then suggested that the duel be postponed, but again Somers refused. Somers was forced to hold his pistol in his left hand, and as a result missed his second opponent completely, while receiving a ball in his thigh, which, while only a flesh wound, occasioned much loss of blood.

When the third midshipman arrived Decatur, now seriously concerned for his friend's weakened condition, again pleaded a postponement, or permission to take Somers's place and fight in his stead, but in vain. At length, Somers found his way unsurely to his mark, where he tottered and fell from loss of blood. He was revived, but found he was too weak to stand, and insisted on fighting from where he sat. Having seen how ineffectual he was as a left-hander, he determined to switch hands again, despite the fact that his right arm was so enfeebled he could not hold his pistol firmly. Decatur, in order to keep his friend's body and arm steady, sat down to his left side, put his right arm around him, and placed his hand under Somers's wavering right elbow. Somers fired and by some fluke managed to wound his adversary.

At this point all parties were prepared to admit that honor had been served, and the challenged midshipmen made suitable acknowledgments to that effect. The matter was closed, and over the succeeding days each took turns nursing the recuperating Somers back to health.

The first duel in which Decatur participated as a principal took place in July 1799, a few months after Somers's multiple confrontation. While the details of the encounter are nowhere near as outlandish as those of the earlier event, they demonstrate even more clearly the powerful hold that the practice of dueling had on the early navy. The fight occurred shortly after Decatur, now twenty years old, had been commissioned and was serving as fourth lieutenant in the *United States*. While the ship was reprovisioning at Chester before returning to sea he was sent upriver to Philadelphia to enlist a few additional crewmen. Following the usual practice, he set himself up at a waterfront rendezvous and advertised the fact that he was recruiting hands. The terms of employment called for a one-year enlistment and included a bounty, payable on signing the shipping articles.

In due course he managed to sign up the requisite number of seamen, and in each case paid out the promised bounty. He was preparing to close up his operation and escort his new recruits downriver when he discovered that some of them had gone off with the mate of an Indiaman, who had offered them higher wages and a bigger bonus to ship on his vessel, which was preparing for a voyage to the Far East.

The furious Decatur stormed onto the Indiaman, waving the signed articles as proof of the prior commitment of his recruits, and demanded their return. The chief mate quickly lost his temper and, employing the usual language of the docks, shouted insults at Decatur and at the service in which he was engaged. Decatur remained cool, and eventually, because he had the signed articles in hand and therefore had the law on his side, managed to collect his men and carry them off.

There the matter might have ended, but Decatur, unsure of his next move, sought out his father for advice. Had his honor been traduced by the Indiaman's mate? Must he seek satisfaction? These were not frivolous questions to either father or son. The senior Decatur took the issue of honor with utmost gravity. Years earlier he had come up with a family motto—*Pro libertate et patria dulce periculum*—and it was of great importance to him that any advice he might give his son would reflect not only the general precepts of honor, but also the very personal ones he had expressed for his family in his schoolboy Latin, which could be translated, "Sweet is the peril in defending liberty and country."

After listening to the details of the younger Decatur's encounter and ruminating on the matter, the father decided the issue was simply too serious to be ignored. As a matter of chivalry, he told his son, he must demand a retraction and be prepared to fight a duel. It was a powerful statement of values: A loving father was prepared to sacrifice his son over a heated insult from a total stranger, all in the name of honor. It was a decision with almost biblical resonance, a dark parody of the story of Abraham and Isaac. In accordance with his father's advice, Decatur sent Dick Somers as his second to demand an apology. When it was refused, a challenge was sent, which was accepted.

Decatur's ship had by that time dropped farther down the Delaware to New Castle, preparatory to sailing, while the Indiaman's mate was still with his ship in Philadelphia. By the terms of the *code duello* an accepted challenge was a binding contract, and should the two men fail to settle their differences before their vessels departed, their meeting would simply be postponed for a year or two. But as it happened the Indiaman was soon ready for sea as well, and when she too dropped down to New Castle and

anchored near the *United States,* her mate came on board at the first opportunity and, asking for Lieutenant Decatur by name, announced that he
was ready to accept his invitation. Decatur immediately prepared to
accompany him on shore. Before leaving he told Charles Stewart, the
ship's first lieutenant, that since he presumed his opponent was not expert
in the use of arms, he would carefully avoid taking his life and would
shoot him in the hip. In the ensuing duel Decatur performed as promised
and wounded his opponent precisely where he had said he would, while
he himself was unhurt.

The undeclared war with France, which was being fought entirely at sea
and confined almost exclusively to the West Indies, continued into 1800.
In spite of the almost continual presence of the USS *United States* in the
Caribbean, Decatur found few chances to distinguish himself in action.
But if his first years at sea were unrewarding in terms of personal satisfaction, they helped mold and define him. By the end of his tour he was no
longer an immature youth but a seasoned officer, and judging from the
description given by an impressionable new midshipman, Robert T.
Spence, an uncommonly promising one:

> *The first time I had the pleasure of seeing [Decatur] was in the West
> Indies, during our differences with the French republic. He was then a
> lieutenant on board of one of our largest frigates, whose officers had
> been selected from among the most promising in the navy, and were, on
> the occasion to which I allude, generally on the quarter deck, grouped,
> as is the custom, in different places, conversing on the various subjects
> of their profession. I was introduced to many of them. They were pleas-
> ing, gentlemanlike men, having the characteristic air and look of
> sailors. But in Decatur I was struck with a peculiarity of manner and
> appearance, calculated to rivet the eye and engross the attention. I had
> often pictured to myself the form and look of a hero, such as my favorite
> Homer had delineated; here I saw it embodied.*

On being released by a kind of spell by which he had riveted my attention, I turned to the gentleman to whom I was indebted for the introduction, and inquired the character of Decatur. The inquiry was made of a person to whose long experience and knowledge of human nature the inward man seemed to be unfolded. "Sir," said he, "Decatur is an officer of uncommon character, of rare promise, a man of an age, one perhaps not equalled in a million!"

Even if we discount the effusive high diction of Spence's description, we can begin to discern an exceptional young leader, still only imperfectly aware of his effect upon those around him.

The Quasi-War dragged on for another year, until Napoleon finally decided that the continued conflict with America might interfere with his plans for developing the Louisiana territory, at which point he ordered his diplomats to negotiate a treaty of peace, resulting in the Convention of Mortefontaine, which was eventually ratified by the Senate in 1801.

As a direct result of America's conflict with France the navy had grown from virtually nothing to a fleet of fifty ships manned by over five thousand officers and men. It was now a respectable fighting force, but Congress, always mistrustful of a standing navy and eager to save money, moved swiftly to return the fleet to a peacetime configuration. In quick order, most of the country's warships were either sold or placed in ordinary (in modern terms "mothballed"), and the majority of naval officers were released from the service and reduced to half pay. Of 110 lieutenants, only 39 were retained on the active list. One of those was Stephen Decatur.

But congressional efforts to reduce naval expenses quickly proved to be a false economy. The world continued to be a dangerous place for an ambitious new nation eager to establish its presence in maritime commerce, and no sooner had Napoleon experienced a change of heart than another seagoing bully emerged to take his place. The bashaw of Tripoli, an egregious troublemaker and rapscallion by the name of Yusuf Karamanli, decided on a whim to renounce his treaty with the United States unless the government in Washington increased the annual tribute it had agreed to pay him. Thomas Jefferson, the new president, was angered by Karamanli's duplicity and responded by sending whatever was left of the navy over to Tripoli, with orders to try to cow the bellicose bashaw.

The warships were dispatched to the Mediterranean around June 1, 1801, under the command of Commodore Richard Dale, a veteran of the Revolution. His squadron consisted of three frigates and a schooner. It was a rather modest show of power, but one that Jefferson hoped would be sufficient to intimidate the Tripolitanians and the other Barbary pirates.

Lieutenant Decatur, eager to do some intimidating, sailed in the smallest of the frigates, the USS *Essex,* as first lieutenant under the command of Captain William Bainbridge. Bainbridge, a large, stolid, unimaginative veteran of the merchant service, had the reputation of a harsh disciplinarian. Decatur, in contrast, seems to have been born with a natural sense of authority that made it easy for him to lead others. He rarely found it necessary to resort to disciplinary measures, and his brief but remarkable address to the crew of the *Essex* before her departure made it evident that his style of leadership was likely to be very different from that of the captain.

> *COMRADES—We are now about to embark upon an expedition which may terminate in our sudden deaths, our perpetual slavery, or our immortal glory. The event is left for futurity to determine. The first quality of a good seaman, is, personal courage,—the second, obedience to orders,—the third, fortitude under sufferings; to these may be added, an ardent love of country. I need say no more—I am confident you possess them all.*

The members of the crew, stunned to hear themselves addressed as equals—an absolutely unheard of departure for a naval officer—roared their approval.

On reaching the Mediterranean, Commodore Dale learned that Kara-manli had indeed made good his threat and had officially declared war on the United States by ordering a squad of his soldiers to chop down the flagpole in front of the American consulate. (The usual explanation for this interesting custom is that in a barren land with few trees, a flagpole was a sign of power and authority, and to destroy one was an act of deliberate hostility. Freudians might suggest another interpretation.)

Since President Jefferson had not authorized an attack on Tripoli, Dale limited his squadron to convoy duty, assigning his ships to shepherd American merchant vessels from one port to another. To Decatur, hungry for fame and renown, the situation was frustrating in the extreme, and may well have led to his confrontation in Barcelona that came close to bringing about an international incident.

In the course of convoy duty the *Essex* stopped at Barcelona, where the local officials and other citizens who visited the vessel were impressed by everything they saw on the American man-of-war. They were loud in their praise of her excellent condition, her disciplined crew, and her courteous, well-turned-out officers, all of whom seemed superior to what could be found in their own warships. Predictably, the local Spanish officers were not pleased with such comparisons, and the visiting Yankees were anything but popular with their opposite numbers.

About a week after their arrival, Decatur and some other officers of the *Essex* were returning from an evening on shore when their boat was peremptorily hailed by the Spanish gunboat guarding the harbor. When the Americans drew alongside they were subjected to abusive language and other insults and ordered to identify themselves. It was self-evident who they were, since their boat bore a large American flag, and Decatur took immediate offense at the Spaniards' obvious harassment and discourtesy. After an angry interchange with the senior officer on the gunboat, carried on in a mix of languages, since the Spanish were as shaky in their English as the Americans were in their Spanish, he ordered his oarsmen to "shove ahead." As the Americans departed they were followed by more abuse from the Spanish, and Decatur shouted back that they had not heard the last of him.

The next morning Decatur, in full uniform, returned to the guard boat and demanded to see the officer responsible for the previous night's altercation. When he was told that the man he sought had gone ashore, Decatur replied, "Well then, tell him that Lieutenant Decatur of the frigate *Essex* pronounces him a cowardly scoundrel, and that, when they meet on shore, he will cut his ears off."

It was stylish insult, an unambiguous threat that was impossible to misinterpret, and so deftly phrased as to invoke the imagery of Spain's national sport. Not surprisingly it caused an uproar in official circles. The captain general of Catalonia summoned the American consul to the palace and informed him that a Spanish officer had been challenged by a hothead from the *Essex,* and that the duel must not be allowed to take place. The consul promised to do what he could, and after consulting with Captain Bainbridge, the two of them managed to persuade Decatur to proceed no further.

Congress continued to worry that its commodores on foreign station, once out of direct communication with the government, were likely to get up to all sorts of mischief. One means of keeping the navy on a short leash was to limit the enlistment of crewmen to a maximum of one year. Given the time it took to prepare a ship for a cruise to the Mediterranean, and then to take her across the Atlantic and back, this allowed for only an abbreviated time on station, and put a severe limit on her ability to act in any meaningful way. In consequence of the policy of short enlistments, soon after Commodore Dale's arrival on station the entire American squadron in the Mediterranean was forced to turn around and head back home, having failed utterly to intimidate the bashaw.

On his return in the *Essex,* Decatur was reassigned to a larger frigate, the *New York,* at the special request of her captain, James Barron. Again he would serve as first lieutenant. The assignment was considered a signal compliment, and an indication of his rising reputation in the navy. The *New York* was dispatched to the Mediterranean in September 1802, carrying thirty thousand dollars in gold tribute for the dey of Algiers, an errand that undoubtedly rankled and mortified all the men on board.

It was now clear to the American government that the bashaw and his brethren were not to be intimidated by a handful of warships, and the new Mediterranean squadron, under the command of Commodore Richard Morris, was considerably enhanced in size and weight of metal, and now consisted of seven frigates and a sloop of war. But while the government had sent out a stronger force, it had assigned a much weaker man to command it. Commodore Morris made it clear that he had no plans for risking his ships in an attack on Tripoli by bringing his wife and child with him on his flagship. Once again Decatur and his fellow firebrands were denied the opportunity for combat and were relegated to boring and unproductive convoy duty. Karamanli remained defiant.

America's continuing failure to cope with Tripoli's threats turned the U.S. Navy into something of a laughingstock among the other nations active in the Mediterranean. The open derision of the Yankees' feeble efforts gave rise to increasing embarrassment and hot tempers among the American officers, which in turn led to an epidemic of duels, many of which proved fatal. One of them involved Decatur's brother-in-law, First Lieutenant James McKnight of the marines, who was killed in a duel at Leghorn. Another fight involved Decatur himself, and like the incident in Barcelona it was important mainly because of its international repercussions. It took place on the British-held island of Malta, in February 1803.

The incident developed when Midshipman Joseph Bainbridge, younger brother of William Bainbridge, went into Valetta on liberty with one of his messmates from the *New York*. There they visited the theater, where they became the subject of unpleasant notice and sneering remarks by some British officers who sat near them. One of the Englishmen spoke contemptuously of the feeble American efforts to fight a war with Tripoli. The two young Americans found themselves in one of those complicated quandaries so common in an age of heightened sensitivities. Were the British officers speaking privately among themselves, in which case they were not being deliberately offensive, and American honor was not impugned? Or were they only pretending to speak privately, with their real object being to hold American honor up to ridicule? It was a delicate question that required earnest discussion. The Americans retired to the lobby to decide whether they should take offense at the British comments. They were soon followed by the British officers. The two young Americans, in an effort to keep their discussion private, began walking up and down the lobby as they talked. The loudest and most outspoken of the British officers, who was clearly spoiling for a fight, began walking in the opposite direction, and as if by accident, ran roughly up against Midshipman Bainbridge. The Americans ignored him and continued to pace up and down. Moments later, the British officer bumped into him again, and Bainbridge still chose to interpret the act as accidental. But when it happened a third time, and it became patently obvious that the Englishman was determined to insult him, and that he could no longer ignore him without a loss of face, Mr. Bainbridge knocked the man down. Angry words were exchanged, and it was clear to all that it was now a matter that could only be settled by a call to the field.

The following morning, a British officer arrived on board the *New York* bearing a challenge for Mr. Bainbridge from the Englishman he had knocked down the night before. The challenger proved to be a gentleman of some note, a Mr. James Cochran, private secretary to Sir Alexander Ball, the governor of Malta. Cochran was a young hothead with a reputation as a professed duelist. Bainbridge was a complete innocent, almost totally unskilled in the use of the pistol and so inexperienced a midshipman he was even ignorant of most of the finer points of dueling. He was about to appoint a friend of his to serve as his second, a man as young and naive as himself, when Decatur learned of the incident and sent for Bain-bridge. He explained to the boy that his antagonist was a skilled duelist, who deliberately arranged such incidents for the thrill of the fight, and that he meant to take young Bainbridge's life, which he most surely would do if the two young innocents went out together. Bainbridge's only hope was to have a second who knew something about the business of dueling, and he offered to serve in that capacity. The young midshipman gratefully accepted.

Decatur introduced himself to Cochran's second and accepted the challenge on young Bainbridge's part. He pointed out that as the represen-tative of the challenged party, it was his right to select the weapons and the specific details of the duel. He then chose pistols and fixed the distance at four paces. Cochran's representative blanched. The generally accepted dueling distance was ten paces, or thirty feet. Decatur was demanding that the duelists stand only twelve feet away from each other. The Englishman objected strenuously.

"This looks like murder, sir," he told Decatur grimly.

"No, sir," Decatur corrected him. "This looks like death, but not like murder. Your friend is a professed duelist, while mine is wholly inexperi-enced." Then he offered a compromise. "I am no duelist, but I am acquainted with the use of the pistol. If you insist upon ten paces, I will fight your friend at that distance."

The Englishman thought for a moment, and then sensing a trap, declined the offer. "We have no quarrel with you, sir."

Decatur refused to agree to any modification of his terms, and when the challenger could not bring himself to back down, the parties met at the agreed hour. Decatur gave the word "Take aim," and watched as the duelists, both trying to mask their fear, raised their pistols. There was less than seven feet between the two barrels. Decatur waited until he observed the hand of the Englishman waver unsteadily, and at that moment ordered "Fire!" Incredibly, both shots missed. Bainbridge's ball passed through his adversary's hat. Cochran, so confident at ten paces, missed Bainbridge entirely.

It was up to Cochran, as the one who had brought on the encounter, to pronounce his honor satisfied and the quarrel amicably ended, but the Englishman refused to make such an offer, so the pistols were reloaded for a second round. Speaking privately to Bainbridge, Decatur told him to aim lower if he wanted to live. Once again the combatants took their positions, the word given as before, and this time the Englishman was hit directly below the eye and was dead by the time he hit the ground. Bainbridge, very much shaken, was unscathed.

When word of the duel reached the governor's office, Admiral Ball was livid, and demanded that Decatur and Bainbridge be arrested and held for murder. Commodore Morris refused to hand them over, and hurriedly sent both miscreants on board the frigate *Chesapeake,* which was already scheduled to return home under the command of James Barron. Decatur was furious at missing his chance for action against Tripoli, and stormed about the ship, threatening to resign his commission as soon as he got home. Barron, his old mentor, cautioned him against such a rash step, and by the time the ship reached the Washington Navy Yard on May 26, 1803, a sullen Decatur had relented.

Decatur was by now twenty-four years old, a veteran of five years' service in the navy. Like all the young officers, he was anxious to distinguish himself in combat and frustrated by the lack of opportunities to do so. But Decatur had yet to discover that he possessed a priceless gift common to almost all successful military leaders—he tended to be lucky. Time and again throughout his career he would demonstrate an almost uncanny knack for finding himself in the right place at the right time. This innate talent would be very much in evidence on his return to the Mediterranean later that year, when he would lead his men to the first great triumph of his career, the celebrated action that would lay the foundation for his legend.

FIVE

Glory

On Tuesday, November 1, 1803, Decatur once again passed through the Pillars of Hercules and into the Mediterranean, dropping anchor in Gibraltar after a notably uneventful crossing of thirty-four days from Boston. It had been a little over six months since he had hastily left for home to escape arrest on the charge of murder. Now he was returning in temporary command of the spanking new brig *Argus*, of eighteen guns, and carrying with him thirty thousand dollars in gold and silver for the use of the American squadron and its new commodore, Edward Preble.

Decatur remained in Gibraltar for two weeks, occupied in turning over the *Argus* to his friend and superior, Lieutenant Isaac Hull, and assuming command of the older and smaller schooner *Enterprise,* of twelve guns. It was not until November 12 that Commodore Preble arrived in the harbor on board his flagship, the *Constitution,* and Decatur was able to report to him in person. He had already heard stories from the other officers of the squadron of Preble's determination to bring the war directly to the Tripolitanians, and was much encouraged by the meeting. Preble was an irascible, strongly opinionated Down-East Yankee who made no effort to curb his short temper or hide his aggressive nature. His fighting spirit contrasted sharply with that of his two predecessors, and Decatur and the squadron's other junior officers took heart.

But no sooner had Preble arrived than he disappeared again, setting sail the next day to deliver the American consul to Algiers. Before departing he ordered Decatur to meet him at the new American command post at Syracuse, where he planned to put together his campaign against Yusuf Karamanli. What neither Decatur nor Preble knew at the time was that a disaster had just occurred a thousand miles to the east that would drastically alter the balance of power in the Mediterranean and render all the American commodore's war plans irrelevant.

On October 31, the day before Decatur's arrival at Gibraltar, Captain William Bainbridge was returning the frigate USS *Philadelphia* to her blockading position off the stormy shores of Tripoli. For several days the wind had been blowing strongly from the west, and had driven the ship a considerable distance off station. Now Bainbridge was taking advantage of a fair breeze to run her down toward the town again.

Around nine o'clock in the morning, with the minarets of Tripoli just visible on the horizon, lookouts spotted a vessel inshore and to windward, standing for the harbor. Bainbridge was eager to overhaul the stranger—there was prize money to be made from such captures—but he was initially reluctant to take his deep drafted ship into uncharted waters that might well mask dangerous shoals. But the temptation of a possible capture was too strong to resist, and eventually Bainbridge overcame his doubts and decided to risk it. He gave the orders to make sail and give chase.

Another captain might have been more cautious, but William Bainbridge had his own reasons for taking a more aggressive course. In his five years of active duty he had somehow managed to compile the most woefully lackluster record of any officer in the navy, and he was eager to clear his reputation.

Soon after receiving his commission as a lieutenant, he had been put in command of the USS *Retaliation*. She was subsequently taken by the French, and Bainbridge became the first American naval officer forced to strike his flag to an enemy.

An even greater humiliation lay in store a year later, when he was given command of a frigate, the USS *George Washington,* with orders to deliver an annual tribute of gold and naval stores to the dey of Algiers. After Bainbridge discharged his cargo the dey demanded the use of his ship to carry an embassy to the ruler of the Ottoman Empire in Constantinople. Bainbridge vigorously refused, protesting that American warships could not be used as common freighters by foreign potentates. But Bainbridge had made the mistake of mooring his ship under the guns of the dey's shore batteries. If he attempted to raise anchor and depart in defiance of the dey's demands, his frigate would be blown out of the water. As the realization of his tactical blunder finally became clear, Bainbridge was forced to change his tune. Reluctantly, he gave in and agreed to do the dey's bidding. After loading an exotic cargo of wild animals, harem slaves, and diplomatic representatives into the *George Washington,* the dey then added insult to injury by insisting that Bainbridge replace the American flag at the main truck with the Algierian standard. Again Bainbridge protested, but again he was forced to capitulate. Once more an American officer had been forced to strike his colors, and once more that officer was William Bainbridge.

The navy forgave him in both instances, but Bainbridge was sensitive to the fact that he now had two formidable black marks against his name, and if he wanted to wipe them away it behooved him to improve his record. It was almost certainly such a mind-set that impelled him to take an unwarranted risk that morning, and to give chase to an otherwise unimportant Arab trader.

Bainbridge quickly discovered that chasing that particular quarry and overhauling her were two quite different things. After a frustrating two hours in pursuit, the *Philadelphia* had made only the barest headway, and a little before eleven o'clock, seeing no other chance of overtaking the stranger in the short time that remained before she reached the safety of the enemy harbor, he opened fire with his eighteen-pounders. He continued firing for almost an hour, but it was at long range, and his men scored no hits. Bainbridge continued to be anxious about having committed his ship to uncharted waters and ordered three separate leadsmen to make constant soundings, to insure the frigate did not run aground. The leadsmen regularly reported depths of anywhere from seven to ten fathoms— roughly forty to sixty feet—as the water shoaled or deepened. The

Philadelphia's normal draft was eighteen and one-half feet forward and twenty and one-half feet aft, so the ship seemed in no danger.

By half past eleven the two vessels had moved considerably to the west and the town of Tripoli now lay in plain sight about three miles distant. Bainbridge, concerned that he was still in uncharted waters, decided to give up the chase. He ordered the helm aport to haul her directly off the land and into deeper water, but it was already too late. Even as the ship was coming up fast to the wind, and before she had lost any of her way, she struck a hidden reef and shot up on it, lifting the suddenly motionless frigate five to six feet out of the water.

The disaster had come upon them so quickly that it took a moment for those on the quarterdeck to absorb just how hopeless their situation had suddenly become. To be stranded on such a coast, in plain sight of the enemy and with no other vessel to bring aid, was nothing short of calamitous.

Bainbridge watched the Arab vessel he had so recently been chasing double the edge of the shoal and sail safely into the harbor, apparently interested only in escaping. But others had heard the American guns, and now nine Tripolitanian gunboats came out to investigate. The situation was perilous in the extreme, and Bainbridge recognized there was not a moment to be lost. The little Arab gunboats might appear insignificant in comparison to the looming frigate, but they would be able to attack with impunity as soon as they understood that the *Philadelphia* was immobilized.

In a desperate attempt to lighten ship, the crew began smashing open the water casks and pumping out the flooded hold, and throwing almost all the guns overboard, leaving only a few for defense. The anchors were the next to go, along with the huge, heavy cables that held them. Bainbridge ordered his men to chop down the foremast, which went crashing into the sea, carrying with it all its sails and rigging. But the ship remained stubbornly embedded in the sandy shoal.

By now the Tripolitanian gunboats had come within range, and tentatively opened fire. The Americans answered with the few guns that remained in the ship. For the moment, they were enough to keep the enemy boats at a respectful distance. As yet, the Arabs had no inkling of the desperate conditions on board the *Philadelphia*. The business of lightening the frigate continued for several hours.

By midafternoon it finally occurred to the Tripolitanians that they had the upper hand. They grew bolder and crossed the stern of the frigate, taking a position on her starboard quarter where they could fire at will, while it was impossible for the *Philadelphia* to bring a single gun to bear.

Night was coming on. With every passing minute the gunboats grew still bolder. Other boats were seen approaching from the town. Bainbridge, after consulting with his officers, saw no recourse but surrender, to save the lives of his people. He ordered the ship's signal books destroyed and the ship scuttled. The magazine was drowned, holes were bored in the ship's bottom, the pumps choked. About five o'clock he signaled his surrender. Any captain must lose heart at such a time, but one can only imagine Bainbridge's feelings, knowing that this was now the third time an American warship had been forced to strike her colors, and on all three occasions he was the man responsible.

Commodore Preble did not learn of the loss of the *Philadelphia* until November 24, three weeks after it occurred, when his flagship fell in with the Royal Navy frigate *Amazon* off the coast of Sardinia, and British officers apprised him of all the sorry details. In a single staggering blow Preble had lost half his frigates and a full quarter of his firepower. All his carefully developed plans for humbling Tripoli were suddenly thrown into confusion, and the future of his squadron's Mediterranean cruise looked decidedly grim.

Losing the ship was bad enough, but there were other distressing ramifications that vastly increased Preble's problems. The bashaw now held over three hundred new hostages and could demand almost any ransom within his imagination. He would now be encouraged to continue fighting no matter what the cost. The United States could not ignore the suffering of its own people, and would be forced to take him seriously.

The British had still worse news for Preble. The scuttling of the *Philadelphia* had been handled so hastily and imperfectly that, when a storm raised the water level a few days after the grounding of the vessel, the Tripolitanians had been able to float her off the sandbar on which she had foundered, patch her up, and bring her within the protection of the harbor forts. Then they went back and fished up her guns from where they had been cast overboard and restored them to their carriages, and once more the *Philadelphia* rode proudly on the waves. All she needed was a new foremast and she could become the most powerful vessel in Yusuf Karamanli's fleet, ready to cruise against the Americans as soon as the mild season returned. In the meantime, she lay at anchor in the middle of Tripoli harbor, the most valuable prize ever taken by the Barbary pirates.

"It distresses me beyond description," Preble wrote grimly to the secretary of the navy. "Would to God that the officers and crew of the *Philadelphia* had one and all determined to prefer death to slavery."

Shortly after hearing the dire news, Preble shaped course for his base at Syracuse. Off Cape Passaro he fell in with Decatur's *Enterprise,* bound for the same destination, and in the course of a courtesy visit to the flagship, Preble told Decatur of the *Philadelphia*'s fate. The two vessels arrived in Syracuse in company, and not long afterward they left again, once more in company, headed for Tripoli to reconnoiter the *Philadelphia.*

Once off the North African coast, Decatur left the deep-drafted *Constitution* safely out to sea and ran the little *Enterprise* close in to the coast to scout the harbor and determine the position of the *Philadelphia*. The sight of the frigate, dwarfing every other warship around her, and lying directly under the protection of the bashaw's land batteries, was a sobering vision. Decatur was much moved by the sight. He had strong personal ties to the ship. As a youth he had witnessed her construction only a few city blocks from his home. Later, his father had served as her first captain. Now, suddenly disgraced, she belonged to his country's enemies, ready to be turned into the most formidable terror in the Mediterranean. Having made note of the *Philadelphia*'s location and of the vessels guarding her, he returned to the open sea to fall in with the waiting Preble. After reporting to the commodore, he made a suggestion. He asked to be allowed to take the *Enterprise* into the harbor and destroy the *Philadelphia*. Preble was sympathetic—Decatur's aggressive spirit matched his own—but he rejected the idea as too hazardous. Still, he agreed that some such plan would have to be worked out, and promised Decatur that since he was the first to make the offer, he should be the one to carry it out.

It was during this brief scouting expedition that an apparently minor piece of good fortune fell the Americans' way, when they managed to overhaul and capture the *Mastico,* a small four-gun ketch of sixty or seventy tons, with seventy Tripolitanians on board, including forty-two slaves. She was an older vessel that had already seen much service, and was not likely to bring much in the way of prize money. But at the moment neither Preble nor Decatur was much interested in prize money. They saw a more valuable use for her. She was indistinguishable from hundreds of coastal traders in the western Mediterranean, and could sail into Tripoli harbor without anyone taking notice. She would be the means by which they would destroy the *Philadelphia*.

Once back in Syracuse, Preble had his carpenters examine the *Mastico*. They reported her basically sound and the commodore, using his discretion as squadron commander, bought her into the American navy and renamed her *Intrepid*. Over the month of January 1804, plans for the raid were worked out in greatest secrecy, for fear that word might get back to the bashaw. Winter was the stormy season in the Mediterranean, and the weather continued foul throughout the month. It was not until February 3, 1804, that Preble judged conditions favorable to send the little *Intrepid* in.

As soon as he had his orders, Decatur mustered the crew of the *Enterprise*—most of whom had no inkling of the secret preparations that had been going on for weeks—and outlined the plan that he and Preble had developed for the *Intrepid*. He warned them of the dangers involved, which were very real, and called for volunteers. Without hesitation, every member of the ship's company, officers, men, and boys, stepped forward in a body. The unquestioning enthusiasm of his crew to volunteer for such a hazardous mission remains one of the most telling aspects of the whole venture. It speaks volumes about Decatur's style of leadership, the high morale of his men, and their great trust in him.

Later that day, from the quarterdeck of the *Constitution,* Commodore Preble watched the little *Intrepid* sail off in company with the brig *Siren,* which would serve as her support vessel. The venture was dangerous, and possibly harebrained to boot, but the destruction of the *Philadelphia* was critical to the mission of the squadron, and for all the perils involved it was the best idea that anyone could come up with. He could only hope that not too many brave men would die in the endeavor. "I shall hazard much to destroy her," he wrote to the secretary of the navy, "it will undoubtedly cost many lives, but it must be done."

Preble had bestowed upon Stephen Decatur the greatest gift that was within his power to grant. Now he would see what the young man would do with it.

Late in the afternoon of February 16, 1804, a weatherbeaten ketch, similar to any number of Arab and Maltese traders plying the coast of North Africa, made her way toward the eastern entry of Tripoli harbor. She appeared in need of caulking and a coat of paint, and there was nothing about her to excite the curiosity of the sentries on the guard boats and in the forts that protected the harbor. The nondescript character of the ketch, and the fact that she aroused not the least interest, was just as well for those on board, for had the Tripolitanians been aware of the true nature of the vessel, they would most certainly have made short work of her.

Near her helm stood two men in native dress. They were Stephen Decatur and a Sicilian pilot named Salvadore Catalano, who had been recruited for the venture because he was familiar with the harbor and spoke the patois used by the sailors along the North African coast. There were perhaps another five or six crewmen in native dress visible along with the pair at the helm, but altogether they represented only a small fraction of the boat's company. A dozen or so men lay prone on the deck, hidden behind the bulwarks, and down below another sixty or so volunteers, armed to the teeth, were making the best of it among the water casks and hogsheads of combustibles crammed into the noisome hold.

As night closed in there was still enough light for Decatur to make out the town of Tripoli, two miles to the west, a collection of sun-bleached forts and minarets dominated by the bashaw's palace. In the heart of the harbor loomed the ship they had come to destroy. The *Philadelphia* was moored in such a way as to serve as the harbor's principal defense. She bristled with twenty-eight eighteen-pounder long guns and sixteen thirty-two-pounder carronades. Decatur had to assume that all the guns were loaded and that there might be as many as two hundred Tripolitanians on board, since it would take at least that number to fight the guns. He knew there were another 115 heavy guns in the forts surrounding the harbor and probably fifty more on the cruisers and galleys that lay at anchor within range of the *Philadelphia*.

The Americans hidden in the little *Intrepid* were fully aware of the dangers surrounding them. Their chances of death, dismemberment, and slavery were probably far higher than their chances of a safe return to base, but there was such a glorious aura of derring-do about the enterprise, such a sense that they were participants in a grand storybook adventure, that it buoyed their spirits and crowded out any fears that might otherwise have sapped their enthusiasm.

Decatur had drilled his crew repeatedly on the particulars of each man's assignment—where he was to go once they boarded the *Philadelphia*, what he was to accomplish, how he was to do it. For all his zeal, there must have been a part of Decatur that recoiled at the idea of destroying such a ship. Almost certainly, during the weeks of planning for the raid, he would have at least considered the possibility of trying to save the *Philadelphia*, of manning her helm and bearing her away in triumph from under the noses of the enemy, that she might fight another day. But just as certainly he would have recognized that such a romantic scheme was totally out of the question. The ship was dismantled, and her bowsprit and foremast gone. Under the best conditions, the mouth of the harbor was a difficult passage for such a large ship, and it would have taken a dozen or more whaleboats to tow her to sea. The only practical solution was to burn her.

Behind the *Intrepid*, hovering near the horizon beyond the mouth of the harbor, lay the American brig *Siren*, of sixteen guns, commanded by Decatur's old friend Charles Stewart. Stewart had disguised his vessel as a trader, so as not to attract attention. The original plan, as worked out in Syracuse, had called for a number of the *Siren*'s crewmen to join the *Intrepid* and augment her fighting force. But earlier that day, when the two vessels had first come within sight of Tripoli, it had been important to keep the *Siren* at a distance from the *Intrepid*, so that she would not be seen to be in any way connected with Decatur's ketch. As darkness fell, the wind, which was light from the north-northwest, prevented the *Siren* from closing in as quickly as had been hoped, and by seven o'clock, Decatur decided he could wait no longer. He would have to go it alone and forgo the extra fighters. He ordered Catalano to enter the harbor between the reef and the shoals, and then explained the change in plans to his men, closing with a quotation from *Henry V:* "The fewer men, the greater share of honor." Decatur was by his own admission no scholar, but it is typical of him that he was intimately familiar with the one Shakespeare play that dealt so specifically with honor and its many ramifications, a subject of paramount importance to him.

The original plan called for the attack to take place at ten o'clock, but Decatur had so often experienced the uncertainty of the weather on the North African coast that when he found the wind, which was now light from the north-northwest, cooperating with his plans, he ordered his helmsman to steer boldly onward, directly toward the *Philadelphia*, now visible in ghostly silhouette, illuminated by the cool glow of a crescent moon.

Around nine o'clock the breeze shifted to the northeast and became very light, but proved strong enough to bring them within two hundred yards of the *Philadelphia*. It was now half past nine, and the setting moon, still visible above the horizon, gave them enough light to see that the ship's ports were open, and her guns run out, and that there were a number of sailors on the spar deck. It had been Decatur's intention to run in under her bows and board over the forecastle, but the shift in the wind meant they would have to improvise.

When they got within a hundred yards of the *Philadelphia*, the wind died completely, and they were momentarily dead in the water. The huge bulk of the *Philadelphia* was blocking any wind and leaving the little *Intrepid* becalmed. Eventually the breeze picked up from the opposite quarter, still very light. The change brought the two vessels nearly parallel to each other at a distance of little more than twenty yards, their heads in the same direction, and the *Intrepid* abreast of the larboard gangway of the *Philadelphia*. Some ten or twelve Tripolitanian sailors were looking over the ship's hammock rail.

The ketch was almost within an oar's length of the frigate when there was a sudden warning call from high above in the *Philadelphia,* ordering her to keep away. Catalano answered, explaining that she was a Maltese boat, and had lost her anchors in the late gale under Cape Mesurado. He asked permission to run a warp to the frigate, and ride by her until the following morning when they could get new anchors from shore. The man on the *Philadelphia,* who seemed to be in charge, considered the matter briefly, and then agreed.

He was curious about the brig that had stood in the offing most of the day—the Americans knew he was referring to the *Siren*—and asked Catalano if he knew anything about her. The Sicilian told him that she was the *Transfer,* a former British man-of-war that had been purchased for the Tripolitanians at Malta, and whose arrival was anxiously expected. The man in the *Philadelphia* seemed pleased with the information.

During the conversation, the wind shifted still again, and once more left the ketch, helpless and motionless, right under the frigate's guns. Fortunately, the *Intrepid*'s small boat was still in tow. Crewmen from the ketch, disguised in the same manner as Decatur and Catalano, clambered into it with as little show of haste as possible, and took a line from the *Intrepid* and made it fast to one of the ring bolts of the *Philadelphia*'s fore chains. The unsuspecting Tripolitanians, in a spirit of cooperation, manned one of their own boats and brought a line from the after part of their ship to the *Intrepid*'s boat, gave it to the Americans, who made gruff but incoherent murmurs of thanks, and brought the line back to their ketch. Then those men hidden behind the *Intrepid*'s bulwark began slowly to haul in the rope, bringing them gradually nearer their prey.

Every man on board the *Intrepid* knew precisely where he was to go once they boarded. None of them carried firearms. In accordance with Preble's written orders, they were to "carry all by the sword." The commodore did not want the noise of pistols or muskets to alert those on shore.

As the moment for boarding grew imminent, each man concentrated on the fury to come. Boarding a ship—particularly at night—calls for an extreme form of hand-to-hand combat, not only dangerous but chaotic, the sort of fighting where plans can change in the flick of a saber, and where the confusion of bodies and blades can baffle and terrify even the hardiest of souls. The Americans were dressed in Arab disguises, and in the dark it would be easy to make fatal mistakes. The only means of identification was the watchword "Philadelphia." That alone might save a man from being slaughtered by his own friends.

Whether it was the unusual rapidity of the approach of the *Intrepid* that aroused suspicion or whether the Tripolitanians noted the movement of shadowy figures on the deck is not known, but just as the ketch was on the point of touching there was a startled cry from the *Philadelphia,* "Americanos! Americanos!" Catalano panicked and shouted "Board, Captain, board!" but Decatur saw there was still more than six feet of open water between the two vessels and shouted, "No orders to be obeyed but that of the commanding officer!" His instantaneous response undoubtedly prevented what would have been a debacle. Moments later as the *Intrepid* touched the *Philadelphia,* he shouted "Board!" and sixty men, led by Decatur and Midshipman Charles Morris, scrambled over the channels and rail and up onto the *Philadelphia's* spar deck, and through the gunports onto the main deck below.

Despite the alarm from the *Philadelphia* the surprise was complete, and the terrified Tripolitanians made only a feeble resistance. A few of the more coolheaded managed to remove the tampions from some of the guns, but they never got a chance to fire them. The deadly sabers and tomahawks of the Americans proved irresistible. Decatur first led an attack on the large number of the crew that had gathered on the forecastle. All those who did not jump into the sea were killed. The lower decks were cleared with the same ruthless dispatch, and in five minutes, the ship was in the hands of her attackers.

Despite Preble's ban on firearms, there was no way to stop either side from yelling, and the noise of the fight raised the alarm on shore and in the cruisers and boats lying nearby. The situation remained perilous, and the Americans expected a bombardment at any moment. There was a hurried call for the combustibles, which were instantly passed up from the ketch and distributed to the gun room berths, the cockpit, the berth deck rooms, and the forward storerooms. The men were supplied with short lengths of sperm oil candles, and at a shouted order from Decatur they set fire to the combustibles. The oily rags and old ropes roared instantly into a blaze, and flames began spilling wildly out of the spar deck hatchways and gunports. So rapidly did the flames spread that the little *Intrepid* was in danger of catching fire as well. Decatur, making sure that everyone was off the burning frigate, was the last to leave, leaping into the rigging of the ketch as she swung away from the blazing *Philadelphia.*

It had taken only about twenty minutes to capture the frigate, set her on fire, and return on board the *Intrepid.* Not a single American life had been lost, and only one man slightly wounded. Some twenty Tripolitanians had been killed outright. Undoubtedly others, who had hidden themselves below decks, died in the flames, while some of those who leaped into the sea probably drowned. At least one boat full of enemy sailors escaped in safety to the town. Only one prisoner was captured. After being severely wounded, he jumped on board the *Intrepid,* where his life was spared by Surgeon Lewis Heerman.

The expedition had been a spectacular success so far, but they were by no means out of danger. Sparks and fragments of fiery canvas floated about everywhere, threatening to ignite the additional barrels of highly flammable combustibles on the *Intrepid*'s quarterdeck. The first order of business was to get away from the burning frigate, but as they raised the jib to catch the wind, the ketch was suddenly sucked back toward the inferno. The huge blaze was devouring all the air around it and creating a vacuum that threatened to pull the *Intrepid* into the fire. It was only by frantic use of the sweeps that they managed to escape from the holocaust they had risked their lives to ignite.

Once safely out of reach of the fire they faced a new danger. The batteries on shore and the cruisers in the harbor began firing at the retreating ketch, but the Americans, intoxicated with their own gallantry, seemed oblivious to the danger. One of the participants, Midshipman Morris, remembered the scene over fifty years later in his memoirs. "While urging the ketch onwards with sweeps, the crew were commenting upon the beauty of the spray thrown up by the shot between us and the brilliant light of the ship, rather than calculating any danger that might be apprehended from the contact."

The sight of the burning *Philadelphia,* in the middle of the small harbor, must have been breathtaking. "The appearance of the ship was indeed magnificent," Morris remembered. "The flames in the interior illuminated her ports and, ascending her rigging and masts, formed columns of fire, which, meeting the tops, were reflected into beautiful capitals."

The town itself was equally spectacular to see. The castles, forts, and minarets were all lit up by the splendor of the conflagration, and shone like an illustration out of the *Arabian Nights.*

The *Philadelphia*'s loaded guns were in the midst of the fire, and as their metal heated, they fired haphazardly from either side. Her starboard battery, which was aimed directly at the shore, smashed blindly into walls and doorways. When the frigate's anchor cables burned through and parted, the *Philadelphia* drifted slowly and grandly toward the town, an aimless funeral pyre and a hazard to every vessel in its path.

The breeze picked up and moved the *Intrepid* toward the harbor mouth, but the guns from the forts and the warships in the harbor continued firing. The shot fell thickly about her, but with little accuracy. One ball passed through her topgallant sail, the only hit. Near the entrance to the harbor, the *Intrepid* was met by the boats from the *Siren,* and together the victorious Yankees made good their escape. By six in the morning the two vessels were forty miles north of Tripoli. From the deck of the *Siren,* the light from the burning frigate was still visible.

Two days later both vessels returned in triumph to Syracuse and an ecstatic Commodore Preble. He ordered a glorious celebratory dinner for the heroes, and within days the raid was the talk of the Mediterranean. When Admiral Nelson heard the story on board his flagship *Victory* off Toulon, he roared with laughter and pronounced it "the most bold and daring act of the age."

Commodore Preble wasted no time in getting off a recommendation to the secretary of the navy. "Lieutenant Decatur is an officer of too much value to be neglected. The important service he has rendered in destroying an enemy's frigate of forty guns, and the gallant manner in which he performed it, in a small vessel of only sixty tons and four guns, under the enemy's batteries, surrounded by their corsairs and armed boats, the crews of which stood appalled at his intrepidity and daring, would, in any navy in Europe, insure him instantaneous promotion to the rank of post captain. I wish, as a stimulus, it could be done in this instance; it would eventually be of real service to our navy. I beg earnestly to recommend him to the President that he may be rewarded according to his merit."

It would take many weeks for the news of Decatur's triumph to reach America, but when it finally arrived his life would change forever. From that day on, presidents would seek out his company. Strangers, speaking in deferential tones, would point to him on the street. At gatherings, voices would drop and conversations pause when he entered a room. Every schoolchild in America would know his name, and countless little boys would reenact the burning of the *Philadelphia* and vie for the privilege of leading the boarding party. Stephen Decatur, still only twenty-five years old, had found the fame and potential immortality for which he had so long yearned. For the rest of his life, he would be a man apart.

SIX

Legend

I f the burning of the *Philadelphia* brought Decatur's name to the attention of the world, his next appearance off Tripoli half a year later
would confirm his reputation as a daring sea warrior of the first rank.

The date was August 3, 1804, and ranged before the walls of Tripoli
was the entire American squadron, consisting of Commodore Preble's
flagship, the *Constitution,* of 44 guns, the brigs *Siren,* 16, *Argus,* 16, *Scourge,*
14, and the schooners *Vixen,* 12, *Nautilus,* 12, and *Enterprise,* 12. The commodore, after having overcome innumerable problems of bad weather,
local politics, and resupply, was finally ready to bring the war home to
Yusuf Karamanli, and in his words, "to beat the Bashaw into a better
humor."

Along with the American warships, Preble had also brought with him
eight little vessels that he had managed to borrow from the king of Naples,
who also happened to be at war with Tripoli. These additions to the
squadron consisted of six twenty-five-ton flat-bottomed gunboats, each
manned by a crew of about fifty men, and two thirty-ton bomb ships, similar in size and design. Each gunboat carried a long twenty-four-pounder
in its bow, and the bomb ships were each armed with thirteen-inch brass
mortars for firing large explosive shells at land targets. These little Italian
boats were shallow-draft vessels that could move in closer to shore than
the American vessels, but they were otherwise hardly more than clumsy
barges, and they had proved to be unseaworthy and difficult to handle
under either sail or oar. They were, however, the best that Preble had been
able to secure. They had been specially refitted in Syracuse and brought
with great difficulty to Tripoli, barely surviving the storms on the voyage
south. The king had provided ninety-six Neapolitan bombardiers and

sailors to help man the boats, and Preble, not knowing exactly what use to make of seamen who could not understand English, and might therefore prove a considerable problem in the heat of battle, distributed them more or less evenly among the gunboats and bomb vessels.

The port they had come to attack was well protected, virtually self-sufficient, and largely immune to either direct attack or blockade. The city of Tripoli was completely surrounded by thick walls, except on the side facing the harbor, which was protected by a series of strong forts and castles, heavily armed. The newest of the batteries, still incomplete, was named the American Fort, because it was being built by the slave labor of the crew of the *Philadelphia*.

Moored in the harbor, supporting his land-based artillery, the bashaw had a ten-gun brig, two eight-gun schooners, two large galleys, and nineteen gunboats. These various vessels were manned by about twelve hundred men. Measured in terms of weight of metal, the American squadron could not match that of the Tripolitanians, but the discrepancy was not particularly significant. The real problem lay in the fact that the biggest and most powerful American guns were on board the *Constitution,* and the dangerous shoals prevented Preble from bringing her close enough to shore to do as much damage as they otherwise might. Even the smaller American vessels were forced to remain offshore, with a consequent loss of accuracy, and therefore, effectiveness. This meant that the main American attack would have to come from the two borrowed bombships, protected by the gunboats.

Preble had separated the gunboats into two divisions, one under the command of Lieutenant Richard Somers, who would lead boats captained by Lieutenant Blake of the *Argus* and Lieutenant James Decatur, Stephen's younger brother, of the *Nautilus*. Stephen Decatur would command the other division, leading boats skippered by Lieutenant John Bainbridge of the *Enterprise* and Sailing Master John Trippe of the *Vixen*. Decatur and Somers had been commissioned on the same date, but because Somers's midshipman's warrant predated that of Decatur, he was recognized as the senior officer of the two and was in consequence put in command of the boats to the right, or western side, while Decatur was in charge of the more easterly division. Such niceties of rank were a matter of great concern among the officers of the early navy, although it is unlikely either Somers or Decatur thought much about it. There was more than a touch of irony in the situation because everyone knew that Preble had recommended Decatur be promoted to captain, which would jump him over seven other lieutenants—including Richard Somers—who were senior to him. Unbeknownst to the squadron, President Jefferson had already acted on Preble's recommendation, and Decatur's new commission was at that moment heading east on board the frigate *John Adams*. Since it would not reach the squadron for several more days, Decatur remained of lesser rank to Somers for the nonce.

The harbor at Tripoli was an ill-defined anchorage protected on its northern side by a line of rocks that ran in an east-west course and served as a natural breakwater, giving the port two entrances. The American squadron had assembled in the open sea to the north of the rocks, opposite the western entrance, which was the one closer to the city, and was the target for the day's operations. The six gunboats and two bomb ships were opposed by nineteen enemy gunboats and two galleys, most of which were positioned outside the rocks in anticipation of the attack. A third division, held in reserve, could be seen behind the rocks, ready to come to the support of the other two.

At two o'clock in the afternoon the entire American squadron moved forward. The six gunboats were cast loose, along with the bomb ships. The larger ships prepared to direct their fire at the enemy batteries and forts, while the bomb vessels, under the protection of the gunboats, moved forward to throw shells into the city.

The numerical odds were stacked against the Americans, both in numbers and in force, since the Tripolitanian gunboats were considerably stronger. But it quickly became apparent that the enemy advantage in the ensuing battle was to be even greater.

As so often happens in combat, a number of things went wrong right from the start. Because of a shift in wind, Somers was unable to sail his gunboat far enough east to give Decatur any support, even with the assistance of sweeps. Then, in the confusion of the attack, the signalman on the *Constitution* ran up the wrong flag, and as a result one of the other boats under Somers's command missed the battle altogether. Then early in the engagement one of the boats in Decatur's division had her lateen yard shot away. She could not be brought alongside an enemy vessel, and eventually grounded on the rocks.

Of the three boats in Somers's division, only the one commanded by James Decatur was able to get up to windward, where he fought with distinguished gallantry. With the effective loss of half of the American gunboats, the odds had thus been raised to about three to one in favor of the Tripolitanians, and the outcome of the engagement was left in the hands of the two Decatur brothers and a third boat commanded by Sailing Master John Trippe.

The three boats continued to advance and were soon swallowed up in the smoke of battle. The Americans fired round shot as they approached the enemy boats, and once within point-blank range swept the enemy's deck with a deadly canister shot of 432 musket balls that acted like an immense shotgun. Those left standing after such a barrage would then have to defend themselves against an American boarding party.

Stephen Decatur led the attack. He kept steadily advancing, delivering as rapid a fire as possible, until his boat came alongside one of the largest of the enemy craft. What happened next, when the Americans caught up with the enemy gunboats, quickly turned into a spectacular scene of carnage and hand-to-hand battle that was more like something out of an Icelandic saga than warfare as it was practiced in the age of gunpowder. Decatur jumped on board the enemy boat, followed immediately by his entire American crew, a screaming, yelling swarm of sailors wielding pikes, swords, and tomahawks. The sailors who had been furnished by the king of Naples remained on board the gunboat. The Tripolitanians, who had been assured by the bashaw that they need not fear the Americans because they were "a sort of Jews, who have no notion of fighting," were terrified by the Americans' unexpected aggression, and retreated to the other side of a large hatchway in the middle of their boat. As soon as Decatur had all his men on board, he charged the enemy round each side of the hatchway. A bloody hand-to-hand fight followed with pistols, cutlasses, pikes, and axes. Many of the Tripolitanian defenders jumped overboard and swam for the rocks. In a few minutes the Americans had killed sixteen and wounded fifteen of the enemy. Only five of the Tripolitanian crew remained unhurt. They surrendered in short order, and the prize was taken in tow.

Simultaneously with this action, Trippe led a boarding party onto another enemy vessel, under even more perilous circumstances. Before most of his men could clamber on board, their own boat lost contact and fell away, and Trippe and just ten of his men found themselves alone on the enemy craft with no choice but to conquer or die. With a roar, they plunged into the massed enemy. Again, the unexpected violence of their attack took the Tripolitanians completely by surprise. Within minutes, Trippe and his men had killed fourteen and captured twenty-two Tripolitanians, seven of the latter being wounded. Trippe did not lose a single man, though two of his crew were wounded and he himself received eleven wounds.

Trippe made only one mistake. While his newly captured prize was being hauled off, he forgot to lower her Tripolitan flag. She was heading triumphantly toward the American squadron with the enemy's ensign set, and the *Vixen*, not recognizing her as a prize, fired a broadside into her that brought down her colors, mast, lateen yard and all. Fortunately, no one was hurt.

Meanwhile Decatur's younger brother James had attacked still another enemy gunboat, which quickly lowered her colors in surrender. The Americans came alongside to take possession, but as the young lieutenant prepared to board his prize he was mortally wounded by the treacherous Turkish captain—all the officers of the gunboats were Turks—and fell into the sea. His men pulled him out and his second in command, a midshipman, drew off and went in search of Stephen Decatur's boat amid the swirling confusion of battle. He found her just after Decatur had completed his capture and was preparing to attack another gunboat. His blood was already up and on hearing the news of James, he flew into a towering rage. Leaving a part of his crew on his prize, he immediately set forth with the remainder of his men determined to avenge his brother.

Blinded by fury and heedless of personal danger, he bore down recklessly on the Tripolitanian gunboat that he thought might be the one he wanted, and jumped on board her before the two vessels touched. He spotted the captain, a large and powerful man, and rushed at him with his unsheathed cutlass, still stained with the gore of his first fight. The Turk carried a long boarding pike pointed with iron. As they met, the Turk thrust it at Decatur, who slashed at the pike with all his might, hoping to cut off the iron point. Unfortunately his cutlass struck the iron instead of the wood, and broke off at the hilt. Decatur was left temporarily disarmed, and the Turkish officer managed to wound him slightly in the arm and chest. Before the Turk got a second chance Decatur grabbed hold of the pike and succeeded in wresting it from him. The two men grappled, and after a terrific struggle fell heavily to the deck.

Decatur managed to land on top of his man, and the two grappled furiously. They were surrounded by their respective crews, each group of men fighting furiously to rescue their commanding officer. In the midst of the struggle another Turkish officer aimed a blow with his scimitar at Decatur's head, which would almost certainly have killed the American had he not been saved by one of his own men who, wounded in both arms and seemingly incapable of protecting his leader, deliberately stepped between the struggling Decatur and the descending scimitar and in an act of almost unparalleled bravery took the glancing blow on his own head. Because the sailor was standing, he was able to intercept the sword at the top of its trajectory, before it had achieved its full force. Though he sustained a dangerous head wound, miraculously, it did not kill him.

Decatur was still in utmost peril. He continued wrestling with the enemy captain, who was much larger and stronger, and who eventually was able to turn him over and get on top of him. Then, holding Decatur down on the deck with his left hand, he drew from his belt a Turkish knife, or yataghan, and was about to kill him when a desperate Decatur seized the hand that gripped the knife and managed to put his other hand into his own pocket and draw out a loaded pistol. Reaching over the huge Turk, he pressed the muzzle into his back and fired down into him, killing him instantly. "It was just like Decatur," declared his old classmate, Charles Stewart, after hearing the details from Decatur himself. "The chances were ten to one that the bullet would pass through both their bodies, but luckily it met a bone and the huge barbarian rolled off dead."

The death of the Turkish officer brought the battle to a close. With their leader and sixteen others killed, the seven survivors of the crew, four of them wounded, soon gave up the fight, and Decatur and his weary men stood as victors on the deck of their second prize.

Around half past four in the afternoon a shift in the wind made further fighting unprofitable, and Preble made the signal for the gunboats to return to the squadron. It had been a small but glorious victory. The bashaw had suffered the loss of six of his gunboats, three sunk and three taken in prize, as well as forty-seven men killed and forty-nine taken prisoner. The Americans had not lost a gunboat, and except for the mortally wounded James Decatur, who would die later that day, had suffered only six wounded.

After the action, Decatur wrote to his friend, Purser Keith Spence: "I found that hand to hand is not child's play. . . . Some of the Turks died like men, but much the greater died like women."

In a wry comment on the Neapolitans in his crew, who had remained in their gunboat, he wrote, "I had eighteen Italians in the boat with me, who claim the honor of the day. While we were fighting, they prayed. They are convinced we could not have been so fortunate unless their prayers had been heard. This might have been the case."

There was one last matter to take care of, and that was for Decatur to acknowledge his debt to the sailor who had selflessly stepped between him and certain death from a scimitar blow. He was a man named Reuben James, a quarter-gunner and a longtime navy veteran who had been with Decatur in the action against the *Philadelphia*. At the earliest opportunity Decatur visited him on board the *Enterprise* where he was recovering from his massive wounds, and after thanking him for his extraordinary act of bravery, asked him what possible favor he might grant him in return. Reuben James furrowed his brow, and after a short pause, answered thoughtfully, "Nothing sir, but to let somebody else hand out the hammocks to the men when they are piped down. That is a sort of business that I do not exactly like."

Decatur nodded solemnly, and promised to take care of it.

While the military value of the August 3 action was limited, it provided an instance of supreme courage and desperate fighting zeal that stands unsurpassed in American naval annals to this day. Further, it gave the American public an unforgettable picture of Stephen Decatur, an iconic image as powerful and precise in its attributes as the holy images of early Christian martyrs. Time and again in future years he would be depicted in popular prints and paintings as the hero lying on the deck of an enemy gunboat, his broken and useless saber beside him, desperately holding off his villainous Turkish assailant while he prepares to dispatch him with his pistol, while looming threateningly overhead another Turk wielding a scimitar is thwarted by a self-sacrificing sailor willing to give his life to save his beloved commander.

Already a hero, Decatur was now the stuff of legend.

SEVEN

Susan

As the frigate *Congress* made her way past the Virginia capes and dropped anchor in the familiar waters of Hampton Roads, her captain, Stephen Decatur, stood on her quarterdeck and looked out upon his native land for the first time in two years.

The date was November 4, 1805, and the long, inconclusive war with Tripoli that had taken him three times to the Mediterranean had finally sputtered to an end, not so much a result of any decisive action on the part of the American navy as to a combination of war weariness and local political unrest that had finally persuaded Yusuf Karamanli to yield to the American demand for a treaty.

His tours in the Mediterranean had been years of high achievement for Decatur. He had won the fame for which he hungered and was returning home a national hero. But there had been a cost. The death of his brother James, so personally painful to Decatur, had been followed soon after by the death of his oldest and closest friend, Dick Somers, who took the little *Intrepid,* loaded with gunpowder, into Tripoli harbor and was vaporized when she exploded under circumstances that have never been satisfactorily explained. Decatur had grieved deeply over these and other lost comrades, and the officer standing on the quarterdeck was a more thoughtful man than the brash young seeker after glory who had departed from Boston in the *Argus.*

In anticipation of his homecoming, Decatur had discarded his normal shipboard attire of comfortable old clothes and a straw hat in favor of a resplendent new uniform, decorated with glittering swashes of gold braid and the twin epaulets of a captain, the highest rank in the United States Navy. His commission, along with a personal letter from President Jefferson expressing his thanks for the destruction of the *Philadelphia,* had arrived only a few days after the first gunboat attack on Tripoli. Decatur had climbed the complete promotional ladder from midshipman to captain in less than six years, and at twenty-five had become the youngest man ever to hold the rank of captain in the United States Navy, a record that stands to this day.

There had been considerable opposition to Decatur's rapid advance. In Washington, Charles W. Goldsborough, the powerful chief clerk of the Navy Department, had argued against the promotion because it would jump Decatur over seven senior officers and set a dangerous precedent. Goldsborough wrote a strongly worded letter to Commodore Preble urging that Decatur be persuaded to decline the promotion. "Such a measure would immortalize him," he wrote earnestly. "The deed would justly bear the character of sublimity—rare instance of the most noble disinteredness. . . . It would be the means of avoiding those bickerings and heartburnings which his promotion will create among those who were his senior lieutenant officers."

It is unknown whether the contents of this amazingly naive letter were ever brought to Decatur's attention. It is unlikely that Preble would have bothered to discuss it with him.

During his voyage home Decatur had played host to a most interesting passenger, a man who now stood beside him on the deck looking out on the Virginia coast. He was His Excellency Sidi Solyman Melimeli, the diplomatic envoy of the bey of Tunis, who was on his way to Washington to establish a permanent representation. Melimeli and Decatur had of necessity been thrown together a good deal during the voyage, and Decatur had come to know and admire the diplomat in the course of their many long conversations. Melimeli was a knowledgeable, worldly man of considerable charm, with a subtle mind and wide interests. Years of diplomatic service had schooled him in the nuances of negotiation and the art of bridging difficult linguistic and cultural differences. Decatur, trained only to iron and gunpowder, had come to appreciate the interesting parallels between his own profession as a warrior and that of diplomats such as Melimeli, and to recognize his own deficiencies, and his need to do something about them. He could foresee that his exalted new status was likely to bring him opportunities in the coming years, but given his lack of schooling would he be able to grasp them? He had reason to wonder.

Decatur was anxious to get home. He had important personal matters to deal with in Philadelphia, but his responsibility to the navy and his distinguished passenger obviously had priority. The *Congress* would remain in Hampton Roads for ten days or so, after which time Decatur planned to deliver Melimeli to Washington, pay off his crew, and leave his frigate at the navy yard to be dismantled and placed in ordinary. Only then would he finally be able to head north.

One of the first visitors to come on board the *Congress* on her arrival in Hampton Roads was Decatur's old commander, Captain James Barron, who made his home locally in the town of Hampton. The two old comrades greeted each other warmly. Decatur invited Barron to stay for dinner—in those days the principal meal was commonly taken in the middle of the day—and his guest readily accepted. He had a close, almost paternal interest in Decatur's rise in the world, and would have been eager to hear of his adventures at first hand. Decatur was no braggart, but he was proud of his accomplishments, and like the heroes of ancient Greece and Rome he was not loath to talk about them. It would have been a particular pleasure to relate his exploits to a man who had served as a role model in earlier days.

Another subject of discussion that would almost certainly have come up that day would have been the future of the navy in which they both served. With the end of the war with Tripoli that future was looking problematical. President Jefferson had already decided that without an enemy to fight, he wanted American seapower completely refigured. Instead of maintaining a navy of comparatively large, oceangoing vessels, he proposed replacing most of the present fleet with one made up of little gunboats designed solely to protect the nation's coasts and harbors. Such a radical shift in policy would directly affect the futures of both men.

Naval officers need two talents above all others: first, the ability to fight, and second, the ability to operate and maintain the fleet they command. In essence, an ideal naval officer must be not only a warrior but an administrator. Both skills are critical to the success of the service, but it is only natural that some officers will tend more to the one than the other, and in the two years since Barron and Decatur had last served together in the same ship, their fortunes and their natural abilities had tended to move them in different directions. The older man, whose character had long since manifested itself in a talent for organization, seamanship, and ship's maintenance, stood in singular contrast to the fiery young Decatur, who had emerged as an exceptional fighter.

But if the two stood at opposite ends of the spectrum of naval command, they were still on close, friendly terms, and one subject that Decatur would almost certainly have touched on at dinner that day was his prospects of marriage. We know almost nothing of Decatur's romantic interests at this point of his life, other than the fact that he had them. Marriage could well have carried career implications for Decatur, and was a natural enough subject to bring up with someone he had known so long and so well. We know that on his return from the Mediterranean that year he was already thinking seriously about marriage, but we know absolutely nothing about the identity of his contemplated bride other than that she was a Philadelphian. We do not know her name, nor do we have any knowledge of what sort of understanding she and Decatur might have had concerning their future. Not a letter to or from her, not a single specific reference to her, has survived. But we know that there was such a woman, and that Barron knew of her. In the light of subsequent events, that fact was to take on considerable significance.

The arrival of the *Congress* in Hampton Roads carrying both the celebrated Captain Decatur and the exotic emissary from the bey of Tunis quickly became the talk of Norfolk. Everyone was eager to catch a glimpse of the glamorous visitors, and a grand reception at city hall was arranged to celebrate their arrival.

The day before that event, the mayor of Norfolk, a local businessman named Luke Wheeler, organized a boating party to the roads and arranged to anchor near the *Congress*. The newspapers had reported that the bey's ambassador had brought with him all sorts of gifts for government officials in Washington, including four Arabian thoroughbreds, and Wheeler suggested that he and his guests visit the frigate to view these wonderful things. Everyone enthusiastically agreed. As it happened, neither Decatur nor the ambassador was on board when the visitors pulled alongside the frigate, but at the invitation of the officer of the deck they clambered aboard and took the opportunity to admire the bey's four horses and to view the other gifts, which were on display in the great cabin.

One member of the boating party was Wheeler's vivacious daughter Susan, a strikingly attractive young woman who found the horses and the state gifts of only indifferent interest compared to something else she came across in the cabin—an exquisite little Italian watercolor painting of young Captain Decatur. As she studied the delicately colored portrait of the dashing and romantic hero she wondered how good a likeness it might be, and whether the handsome fellow in the picture already had plans to give it to someone.

The following day at the municipal reception, Susan had an opportunity to meet in person the subject of the painting, and to judge for herself the accuracy of his portrait. Whatever she may have thought of the likeness, she was much taken with the original. Decatur was equally smitten. He had just returned from foreign station after two years, and Susan Wheeler's grace and charm simply overwhelmed him. By the end of the evening, he was hopelessly, helplessly besotted with her.

Susan was not exactly a blushing innocent. Well educated, charming, musically talented, and indulgently spoiled by her rich father, she had long been socially active. She was three years older than Decatur, and had in her time caught the eye of any number of prominent men throughout the Chesapeake region. She had already rejected the advances of Vice President Aaron Burr as well as those of Jerome Bonaparte, brother of the emperor of France.

Susan was also something of a woman of mystery. There were rumors that she was Wheeler's illegitimate child, and had been born in the obscurity of Elk Ridge Landing, Maryland, where her father ran an ironworks. Nothing was known of her mother, but it was whispered in some quarters that she had been a mulatto, a particularly sinister accusation in the antebellum South. If Decatur got wind of any of these stories—and in all likelihood he did—they carried little weight with the lovesick captain.

After their initial meeting, he arranged to see her virtually every day thereafter, until he could delay his trip to Washington no longer. He finally tore himself away on November 23, having confessed to her his Philadelphia commitment and his intention to end it. Such a promise could not have come easily to a man of such rigid standards of honor, but he could see no other answer. He was determined to have Susan.

His stop in Washington was brief but instructive, and provided Decatur with an object lesson in how much he still had to learn about dealing with his new fame. He was hailed everywhere as a conquering hero. Statesmen and dignitaries vied for the opportunity to meet the man who had bested the bashaw. The whole government seemed his to command. While it was undoubtedly gratifying to find himself the center of attention in such august circles, it soon became apparent that his celebrity status was not going to do him much good in terms of getting the government to take any action on a matter of deep personal importance to him.

Decatur and the men who had helped him destroy the *Philadelphia* had confidently expected that Congress would vote them prize money for their exploit. Because of the frigate's inestimable value to the enemy, and the fact that she was relatively new, there was every reason to expect Congress to put a high evaluation on her—perhaps as much as two hundred thousand dollars—and award the full amount to the officers and men who captured her and put her to the torch.

Under the complex formulas of prize law, Decatur's share of such an award would have been gratifyingly large—at least fifteen thousand dollars and perhaps as much as twice that amount, a real fortune in those days—but even the lesser sums that would have accrued to the officers and men would have been highly welcomed by them.

But Congress, instead of bestowing prize money, chose instead to award Decatur a commemorative sword, and voted to each of the officers and crew of the *Intrepid* two months' pay. While the award to Decatur was generally seen as appropriate, if parsimonious, the two months' pay for everyone else was perceived as insulting, and every one of the officers refused it.

Decatur was personally embarrassed by the situation, and when he got to Washington made it a point to raise the question of prize money with those in power. His legal advisor, the Virginia lawyer Littleton Tazewell, urged him as a matter of honor to press his case for prize money "as the guardian and protector of the officers and people associated with him in this daring and honorable enterprise," and while every congressional figure he met seemed to agree to the justice of his case, no prize money was ever awarded.

The reluctance of Congress presented Decatur with a dilemma. He felt strongly that he was in the right, but his rigid concept of gentlemanly behavior inhibited him from pressing his case. It would take another eight years before Decatur finally found a way to bring Congress to heel.

In early December Decatur returned to Philadelphia, where he received another hero's welcome. He had a warm reunion with his family, who by that time had removed to Frankford, just north of Philadelphia, and it was there that he saw for the first time the commemorative sword awarded by Congress. There were celebratory dinners with old comrades, and a particularly affecting reunion with his revered commander, Edward Preble,

and other members of the Mediterranean squadron, including William
Bainbridge, who had at last been freed from his Tripolitanian captivity.
Somewhere during that Christmas season he also managed to break off
his relationship with a certain unnamed young lady.

Through all the festivities, Susan Wheeler remained constantly on his
mind. Mindful of her talents as a musician, he had arranged for his friend
Master Commandant Isaac Chauncey in Norfolk to deliver a gift of sheet
music to her. Chauncey's letter to Decatur, confirming that he had completed his mission, is charming:

> *Sir . . . the commision that you honored me with for Miss W. I delivered
> into her own hands, She blushing received the Music and with looks
> that expressed the feelings of her Soul thanked me as the Bearer but
> more particularly, the* Donor *for not forgetting her—She asked me to
> call the following day, I did so and found the little packet had wrought
> mericles, it had indeed has been Music to her Soul, for Joy beemed in
> her Eyes and her every gesture was heavenly—and I* may *adopt the
> language that* Milton *has put in the mouth of Adam "Grace was in all
> her steps, Heaven in her Eye, in every gesture dignity and love."*

Chauncey reported that Susan seemed particularly interested in the
disposition of the congressional sword awarded to Decatur. She undoubtedly knew it had been sent to his parents for safekeeping, but appeared to
feign ignorance in order to angle for the information she wanted:

> *She was extremely cautious and circumspect in all her inquiries She
> however cou'd not help saying that she had heard that you was to be mar-
> ried on your arrival in Philadelphia, that the Sword presented to you by a
> voat of Congress had been sent to Miss —— of that place for safe keep-
> ing, that you wou'd be obliged to Marry the Lady to save the Sword, I told
> her that the World was generally liberal with what did not belong to them,
> that report frequently disposed of single Gentlemen and Ladies without
> asking their consent, and that it was with you as many others, that report*

had been premature in that particular for I did not believe you had an Idea of marrying any person in Philadelphia, that I knew as far as related to the Sword was not true, for to my knowledge it was forwarded to your father. She however I thought appeared a little Jealous—at any rate my dear fellow you will return this Winter and act your part well, if I mistake not (to make another Quotation from Milton you may say with Adam) "To the Nuptial Bed I led her blushing like the Morn all heaven and happy Constellations on that hour shed their choicest influence" Where I shall leave you my dear friend to make the best use of your time.

There is no suggestion or even a hint anywhere in this delightful and warmhearted letter that it was written by a battle-hardened veteran who had in his day ordered floggings and seen men blown apart before his eyes, nor that it was addressed to a man who had killed with his bare hands and been disappointed by those Turks who "died like women."

Decatur had reached the top of his profession at a particularly young age, and while he might be a natural leader and warrior, he was acutely aware of his intellectual shortcomings. He knew that if he wanted to continue to rise he was going to have to learn new skills, develop new interests, and exhibit a social polish and subtlety he did not as yet possess. It was during his furlough at home that he decided to do something about it. At one point during his stay, Dr. Benjamin Rush, an old family friend, came to visit. Rush, in addition to being a prominent Philadelphia physician, was a signer of the Declaration of Independence, a close confidant of George Washington, and the father of Decatur's old school friend, Richard Rush. Dr. Rush had known Decatur since childhood, and in a letter written many years after the event, Richard Rush recalled a conversation Decatur had with his father that reveals the younger man's determination to capitalize on his newfound prominence.

According to Rush's letter, Decatur approached his father privately, and after some hesitation said:

Doctor, I am going to speak to you as a friend. By good fortune I have risen fast in my profession, but my rank is ahead of my acquirements. I went young into the navy; my education was cut short, and I neglected the opportunities of improvement I had when a boy. For professional knowledge I hope to get along, expecting to increase it as I grow older; but for other kinds of knowledge, I feel my deficiencies, and want your friendly aid towards getting the better of them. Will you favor me with a list of such books, historical, and others of a standard nature, as you think will best answer my purpose, that I may devote myself at all intervals to the perusal of them?

Dr. Rush, impressed by the young man's earnest sincerity, readily agreed to provide such a list, and Decatur from that time on became an avid reader for the rest of his life. Clearly, he was determined not to rest on his laurels, or as Richard Rush observed, "His ambition grew more elevated with his every new achievement."

Toward the end of January 1806, Decatur at last managed to part with his family and get back to Norfolk and to Susan, where the two beautiful, headstrong lovers, freed at last from the constraints imposed by his previous Philadelphia commitment, could fall into each other's arms and abandon themselves to the delights of passionate self-absorption.

In February an incident occurred that in itself might have been innocent enough, but was subsequently seen to take on grave significance. One morning on the streets of Norfolk Decatur happened to run into James Barron and some other mutual navy friends. As they paused on the corner to chat, one of the group, evidently aware of Decatur's interest in Susan Wheeler, asked him teasingly if there were not some "particular attraction" that drew him to Norfolk. Barron objected to what he thought was an improper implication in the jest. Decatur had previously told him of his engagement to a girl in Philadelphia, and Barron made it clear that the young man's affections were already centered elsewhere. The highly sensitive Decatur, caught out on a matter of personal honor, and deeply distressed to be reminded of his previous commitment, reacted strongly to Barron's innocent comment and stormed off, to the utter bewilderment of Barron and his companions.

The story is certainly true, but whether it contributed in any way to the hostility that eventually grew up between the two men remains open to question.

On March 8, 1806, in a ceremony notable among other things for the absence of James Barron from the guest list, the Reverend Benjamin Porter Grigsby, pastor of Norfolk's Presbyterian congregation, married Stephen Decatur and Susan Wheeler. It was to prove a notably warm and vibrant union.

EIGHT

The Leopard–
Chesapeake *Affair*

Early in March 1807, a year after his marriage, Decatur was supervising the construction of gunboats at the Norfolk Navy Yard when he received an official letter from his friend Colonel John Hamilton, the British consul in Norfolk, demanding the return of four sailors who had escaped from British warships anchored in the area. Three of the deserters, the letter claimed, had been recruited into the USS *Chesapeake*, a frigate being readied in Washington for a Mediterranean cruise.

Decatur saw at once that the letter had nothing to do with him, since his responsibilities were limited to the Norfolk Navy Yard. He dashed off a polite reply, explaining that the issue of British deserters lay outside his command, and suggesting that Hamilton take up the matter with the local civil authorities or seek help from the British ambassador in Washington. He then promptly forgot about Hamilton's letter and turned his attention to more pressing business. He could hardly have imagined that this quite ordinary interchange, which involved Decatur in only the most peripheral manner, would presage an explosive international crisis that would rock the United States to its foundations, and would in time, through innumerable twists and turns, contaminate the navy's officer corps and lead directly to his own death years later on the dueling field of Bladensburg.

The chain of events that would bring about such a series of dire and far-ranging consequences had its inception in a naval action between Britain and France that took place far from America and had nothing to do with the United States. On August 11, 1806, a British naval squadron was pursuing some French warships in the Atlantic when a hurricane swept out of the south and scattered the vessels of both navies willy-nilly toward the northwest.

Two of the battered French ships took refuge in Chesapeake Bay. One of them, the *Patriote,* a ship of the line, put in at Annapolis, her topmasts gone and several of her guns thrown overboard. The other, the frigate *Cybelle,* limped into Norfolk. Both ships had suffered considerable damage from the storm, and required extensive repairs. Because the United States was a neutral power, the French ships were safe so long as they remained in American waters, but Vice Admiral Sir George Cranfield Berkeley, commander of the Royal Navy's North American Station, was determined to keep close watch on them. He immediately dispatched a British squadron to take up position at the mouth of the Chesapeake, ready to pounce on the French ships at Annapolis and Norfolk should they try to regain the ocean. It was a formidable squadron, consisting of two seventy-four-gun ships of the line, the *Bellona* and the *Triumph,* along with the frigate *Melampus* and several smaller vessels. The British established anchorages in Hampton Roads and Lynnhaven Bay, four miles inside Cape Henry, at the mouth of the Chesapeake.

The presence of so many British warships in such close proximity to Norfolk made the local townspeople understandably nervous. Many could still remember the bad feelings of the Revolution. But the British made it clear that they had no interest other than keeping a close watch on the French warships, and in time the Americans grew used to them. The ships would regularly send in landing parties to obtain water and supplies, and on occasion the more senior officers would visit the town, without incident.

And then the desertions began.

A small Royal Navy store ship, the *Chichester,* lost several men when she went in for extensive repairs at the Gosport yard.

Others soon followed. The situation grew more critical when the Navy Department in Washington decided to send the frigate *Chesapeake* for a cruise to the Mediterranean, and in order to enlist a crew, set up recruiting offices at various seaports, including Norfolk. The navy was anxious to avoid trouble with the British and laid down strict caveats against enlisting foreign deserters, but the recruiting officers, given the opportunity to enlist some experienced hands who may or may not have been deserters, honored the rule as often in the breach as in the observance, and dissatisfied sailors on the British ships found a convenient place to which to escape.

Desertions increased.

In early March 1807, five men from HMS *Melampus* seized the captain's gig and, in a hail of gunfire, escaped the frigate while she was lying at anchor off Hampton. The men, who had run away on the spur of the moment and were in immediate need of cash, were pleased to discover that the American navy was offering enlistment bonuses to qualified hands. The day after their escape, three of the deserters signed on to the *Chesapeake*.

These were the men that the British consul had mentioned by name in his letter to Decatur. After Decatur had explained that he was powerless to intervene, the consul wrote off to Washington to seek help from the British minister there. But even as he sent off his request, there was another, more flagrant multiple desertion, this time from the sloop *Halifax*. On the evening of March 7, five men seized control of the ship's jolly boat, and taking advantage of the dark and heavy rains, rowed toward shore. Among the escapees was an English tailor named Jenkin Ratford, thirty-four years old, short, slight of build, and easily identified because his name was prominently tattooed on his left arm. All five signed up for the *Chesapeake*. To evade the Navy Department's restriction against enlisting deserters, they all used false names. Ratford, despite his tattoo, entered himself in the books as "John Wilson."

A few days after their escape, the captain of the *Halifax*, Lord James Townshend, ran into one of the deserters on the street in Norfolk, and persuaded him to return to the ship. According to Townshend's testimony, the two men had walked about twenty yards when Jenkin Ratford ran up and pulled his shipmate away from the captain and declared "he would be damned if he should return to the ship; that he was in the Land of Liberty; and that he would do as he liked, and that I had no business with him."

By this time, Colonel Hamilton had sent off his letter to the British minister in Washington, asking for help in getting the *Melampus* deserters back. The minister, David Erskine, took up the matter with Secretary of State James Madison, and Madison in turn bumped it to Secretary of the Navy Robert Smith. Finally, Smith referred it to the officer in charge of the *Chesapeake,* who happened to be Decatur's old mentor Commodore James Barron. The secretary's letter to Barron referred specifically to the men who had deserted from the *Melampus:* "It is represented to me that William Ware, Daniel Martin, John Strachan, John Little and others, deserters from a British Ship of War at Norfolk, have been entered by the recruiting officer of that place for our service." Smith wanted Barron to find out if such men were in fact on the ship, interview them, and report back to the Department.

But the secretary's letter also touched on another sensitive issue: Were the deserters American? A great many American sailors had been illegally impressed into the British navy, and Barron was ordered to look into that question, too: "You will be pleased to make full inquiry relative to these men (especially if they are American Citizens) and inform me of the result."

Barron immediately interviewed the first three named men. (There was no record of John Little, who either chose not to join the others, or may have enlisted under a false name.) He concluded that all three of them had indeed deserted from the *Melampus,* but that they were all Americans. As such, he reported back to Smith, he would not return them to their former servitude.

Barron's findings were referred in turn to Secretary Madison, and from him to the British minister, who passed them on to the consul in Norfolk and to Admiral Berkeley, in Halifax, Nova Scotia. That seemed to close the matter.

Somehow, in all the shuffling of papers, the question of "John Wilson," as Jenkin Ratford called himself, was overlooked by all, with the notable exception of Lord James Townshend, captain of HMS *Halifax*. He had been publicly humiliated by Ratford on the streets of Norfolk, and he could neither forgive nor forget.

Commodore Barron, having finished his business in Washington, returned home to Hampton to spend a last few weeks with his wife and daughters while waiting for the *Chesapeake* to be ready for sea. Barron was not the frigate's captain. His orders called for him to take command of the Mediterranean squadron, and the *Chesapeake* was to serve as his flagship. The actual captain of the frigate, the man in day-to-day command, would be Master Commandant Charles Gordon.

Early in June, Gordon brought the ship down the Potomac and into Hampton Roads for final refitting and provisioning. The day after Gordon's arrival, Barron paid a visit to the *Chesapeake,* and found her upper decks a scene of confusion. She had been deliberately lightened before leaving the Washington Navy Yard as a precaution against running aground on the Potomac's shoals. Only twelve of her guns were mounted, and many of her fittings had been sent down separately for final installation in deeper water. Now that she lay in Hampton Roads, it was safe to complete provisioning and the installation of her heavier equipment. Water casks, lengths of anchor cable, and the rest of her guns were all hoisted on board and put into place.

To add to the disarray, the decks of the *Chesapeake* were also cluttered with the furniture and other personal effects of certain civilians who would be traveling in her on government business. Their goods and possessions, still unstowed and sitting on deck, added to the sense of disorder. Barron, after claiming to be fully satisfied with his brief inspection, left the ship soon after and returned home.

A few days later, he made a second visit. The ship's captain, Charles Gordon, reported that she was almost ready to depart, but that the weather was out of the wrong quarter, and that they were windbound. It was not until Sunday, June 21, 1807, almost three weeks after Barron had first visited the *Chesapeake* on her arrival in Hampton Roads, that the commodore received word that she was finally ready to sail. He immediately came on board and moved into his permanent accommodations in the great cabin.

At seven o'clock the following morning, the *Chesapeake* set sail. Little had been done in the way of clearing the decks, which were still piled high with civilian luggage and lumbered with goods and equipment that required stowing. After clearing the Roads, but still within the Chesapeake, the ship passed the British squadron that lay at anchor off Lynnhaven Bay. Later it was remembered by some of the *Chesapeake*'s officers that the British flagship signaled two other British vessels that were anchored out beyond the Cape Henry lighthouse. One of them was the seventy-four-gun *Triumph,* which had been part of the blockading squadron from the beginning. The other was a recent arrival from Halifax, HMS *Leopard,* a fifty-gun double-decker, somewhat smaller than a true ship of the line, but considerably larger and more powerful than the *Chesapeake*.

A little while later it was noted that the *Leopard* had weighed anchor and moved into open water, in apparent response to the signal from the British flagship. Around two o'clock in the afternoon, the *Chesapeake,* now beyond Cape Henry and in the ocean proper, stood in toward the land in preparation for dropping her pilot. It was noted that the *Leopard* changed course as well, and appeared to be shadowing the American frigate.

At 3:27 that afternoon, the *Leopard,* which had been swiftly approaching the *Chesapeake,* came within sixty yards of the American frigate and hailed her. The British captain called out that he had a dispatch for the Americans. Barron, standing in the starboard gangway with a speaking trumpet in his hand, gave the British captain permission to send a man on board, and ordered the *Chesapeake* hove to.

Strict interpretation of American naval regulations required the commanding officer of a warship to call his crew to quarters when approached by a warship of another power, but Barron was not a by-the-books commander and felt no need for such precautions. Britain and America were at peace, and it seemed a totally unnecessary drill.

A few minutes later, with both ships hove to, and the coast of Virginia only a thin line on the western horizon, a Royal Navy lieutenant was rowed across and, coming on board, handed Barron a note from the *Leopard's* captain, enclosing an extraordinary circular letter from Sir George Cranfield Berkeley, Vice Admiral of the White, addressed to all ships of the British North American Station:

> *Whereas many Seamen, subjects of His Britannic Majesty, and serving in His Ships and Vessels as per margin [the British ships specifically mentioned in the left margin were the* Bellona, Belleisle, Triumph, Chichister, Halifax, *and the cutter* Zenobia] *while at Anchor in the Chesapeak deserted and entered On Board the United States frigate called the* Chesapeak, *and openly paraded the Streets of Norfolk in sight of their Officers under the American flag, protected by the Magistrates of the Town, and the Recruiting Officer belonging to the above-mentioned American Frigate, which Magistrates and Naval Officers refused giving them up, although demanded by His Britannick Majesty's Consul, as well as the Captains of the Ships from which the said Men had deserted, the Captains & Commanders of His Majestys Ships and Vessels under my Command are therefore hereby required and directed in case of meeting with the American frigate* Chesapeak *at Sea, and without the limits of the United States to show to the Captain of her this Order; and to require to search his Ship for the deserters from the before mentioned Ships, and to proceed and search the same, and if a similar demand should be made by the American, he is to be permitted to search for any Deserters from their Service, according to the Customs and usage of Civilized Nations on terms of peace and Amity with each other.*

Barron read the letter in a state of total shock and amazement. It was an absolutely outrageous document. For Admiral Berkeley to claim that he had some sort of authority over an American warship was a degree of arrogance beyond Barron's ability to comprehend. The captain of the *Leopard,* who clearly understood the intemperate nature of Berkeley's letter, had appended a personal note:

> *The captain of the* Leopard *will not presume to say anything in addition to what the Commander in Chief has stated, more than to express an hope, that every circumstance respecting them may be adjusted, in such a manner that the harmony subsisting between the two countries, may remain undisturbed.*

Barron knew all about the three deserters from the *Melampus,* but Berkeley's circular did not even mention that ship. Of any other deserters who might be in the *Chesapeake*'s crew, he knew nothing.

Barron told the British lieutenant that to the best of his knowledge there were no such men as those listed in his ship, and that in any case, under no condition could he allow British officers to search his ship, or carry off members of his crew. He wrote a brief letter to the captain of the *Leopard* to that effect, gave it to the lieutenant, and saw him back to his boat.

Only then, almost an hour after the *Leopard* had first hailed, did Barron think to put the *Chesapeake* in battle trim, and even then his order was couched in the most circumspect manner. He turned to Gordon and said, "You had better get your gun deck clear, as their intentions appear serious." A few minutes later, he was a little more explicit. He ordered Gordon to call the crew to general quarters, but specified that he do so secretly, without beating the drum or opening the gunports, which might alert the British. Everyone on the American ship was aware that the British were already at battle stations, with their guns run out and their tampions—the plugs in their muzzles—removed, ready to fire.

While the *Chesapeake*'s crew scrambled to make up for lost time, the British captain, who by this time had read Barron's note, hailed again. Barron strained to hear him, and asked him to repeat his message. As if to clarify the British intent, the *Leopard* fired a shot across the bow of the American ship. Moments later, to the horror and bewilderment of the Americans, the entire port side of the *Leopard* erupted in a broadside that tore at the *Chesapeake*'s masts and hull, and sent lethal splinters in every direction.

As the *Leopard*'s crews reloaded, the Americans frantically prepared to respond in kind. Men ran in every direction, cursing and shouting for powder horns and matches, struggling to loose their guns, pull out their tampions, set tackle, and somehow find the means to fight their guns.

There was a second broadside from the *Leopard,* and then a third. Desperate *Chesapeake* officers discovered that the gunner's mate had no powder horns to give them, nor matches, nor were there even heated loggerheads to fire the guns.

Barron saw his ship being transformed into a shambles. "Is it possible we cannot get one gun to fire?" he shouted in an agony of despair. He had been wounded in the leg by a splinter and was having trouble standing. "For God's sake, gentlemen, will nobody do his duty?"

Still not one shot came from the American ship. The gun crews tried frantically to get the lumber out of the way so they could work their guns. Finally, from Barron, came a last desperate order: "For God's sake to fire one gun for the honor of the flag, I mean to strike!"

Lieutenant William Henry Allen had somehow managed to prime three guns and was trying to find some means of firing them. Finally, with a pair of tongs, he fished a burning coal from the galley stove at the other end of the deck, and running back to his station, managed to fire one shot. He was about to fire a second when Barron yelled, "Stop firing! Stop firing! We have struck! We have struck!"

Even as he gave the order to lower the flag in surrender, the British fired a last broadside.

Fifteen minutes later, two boats filled with officers arrived from the *Leopard*. Once on board, they ordered the Americans to muster the crew, but

Barron refused. He had struck his colors, he insisted, and thereby surrendered his ship. The British had captured the *Chesapeake* in an act of war. He and all the men on board were prisoners of the Royal Navy. The British officers ignored him and began hunting for deserters. In time, they selected four members of the crew and removed them to the *Leopard*. They were the three Americans from the *Melampus* whom Barron had interviewed in Washington, along with Jenkin Ratford from the *Halifax,* still claiming to be "John Wilson," despite the telltale tattoo.

As the British prepared to return to their boats, Barron insisted they take the *Chesapeake* as prize. They ignored him. Around eight in the evening, the *Leopard* departed to rejoin the rest of the blockading squadron, and the *Chesapeake* was left to find her way back to Hampton Roads.

The following morning, to the astonishment of observers on shore, the *Chesapeake* was sighted off Cape Henry at seven o'clock. News of her presence was immediately dispatched to Norfolk, and Stephen Decatur was among the first to hear the curious and totally unexpected report. He made immediate arrangements to get down the Elizabeth River, and around five o'clock that afternoon, with the *Chesapeake* once again at anchor in Hampton Roads, he went on board.

What he saw shook him to the core. The ship was in a state of chaos. Shattered timbers, dead bodies, civilian trunks and furniture, tubs of beef and other unstored provisions lay about on the deck, a scene of inexplicable carnage. The story of the *Leopard*'s attack was quickly told. There was a general anger at British perfidy, but Decatur did not allow himself the luxury of such posturing. There would be time for that later. All other details paled to insignificance beside the shocking fact that Commodore James Barron had surrendered without a fight. That an American officer could allow a ship of the U.S. Navy to be so dishonored was almost beyond imagination. To Decatur's eyes, it was an outrage that had to be avenged.

NINE

Court-Martial

News of the *Leopard*'s attack on the *Chesapeake* unleashed a storm of fury across the United States. Unlike Decatur's anger, which was centered on Barron's inaction, his countrymen's outrage was focused almost entirely on the British attack. Angry crowds gathered in seaports up and down the coast to protest the latest incidence of the Royal Navy's arrogance. As news of the casualties spread—three killed, eighteen wounded (one of whom would later die)—there were furious calls for war and retaliation. A nervous Thomas Jefferson, who knew that America could not possibly survive such a war, characterized the popular reaction as "a state of excitement in this country not seen since the battle of Lexington."

In Norfolk, at the epicenter of the crisis, there was rioting in the streets. John Hamilton, the British consul, a longtime resident with many friends in the city, reported to his government that "it is impossible to describe the popular agitation and irritation which have prevailed at this place since the return of the *Chesapeake* to the Roads." Citizens of Norfolk and neighboring Portsmouth unanimously adopted resolutions calling for an end of all communication with, or assistance to, the British warships blockading Chesapeake Bay.

Four days after the attack the commander of the British squadron, disdainful of the angry rabble on shore, sent the schooner *Hope* into Norfolk carrying Lieutenant Manderson of the *Bellona* with dispatches for Consul Hamilton. The lieutenant came on shore in a boat and went directly to the consul's home. Within minutes a crowd of about a hundred shouting, angry men besieged the place, "insisting in the most clamorous and violent Manner that the British Officer should be given up to them," Hamilton reported, "as an Atonement for the Blood shed on board the *Chesapeake*."

While the authorities, including Decatur, tried to reason with the crowd, some of the mob dragged Manderson's boat into the streets to prevent his escape. It was only after considerable effort that Decatur and the city officials managed to calm the crowd, and the British lieutenant was allowed to return to his ship.

Strong anti-British sentiment continued to run high for weeks, and the *Norfolk Gazette and Publick Ledger* indignantly explained why: "The *Chesapeake* is lying in Hampton Roads without any colours! And strange to tell the *Leopard* is triumphantly riding at anchor within our waters near the Capes!"

One of the first moves by Secretary of the Navy Smith was to relieve Barron of his command of the *Chesapeake,* and to order Decatur to take his place. At noon on July 1 Decatur formally took command. Four hours after he came on board, Barron left the ship in stony silence. His right leg had been cut up in the action, and he limped noticeably as he walked stiffly past the ship's junior officers lined up at attention to see him off.

By July 4, Decatur and his navy yard constructor had inspected every inch of the *Chesapeake* in detail, and he was able to send Secretary Smith a specific damage report. She had taken thirteen round shot in her hull, he noted, considerably less than the twenty-two previously reported, and "can be repaired in four days by six carpenters." The spare fore topmast was found to be "entirely unfit for service," and of her boats the second cutter was "much injured," and the first cutter was "slightly injured." Both mizzen- and mainmasts were "irreparably" damaged, but the foremast, which had been struck by one shot, could be repaired. Seven of the fore and main shrouds as well as the main and spring stays had been cut away, but could be repaired. The mizzen rigging was beyond repair. The frigate could be completely repaired in three weeks.

For several days following the incident, the British behaved as if they were the wronged party, and sent insolent and menacing messages in to Norfolk, declaring that if the people maintained their boycott and did not supply them with such articles as they might want, the British squadron would come up and retake the *Chesapeake* and cut out the French frigate *Cybelle,* to boot.

Apparently they meant to do just that. On July 3, the four largest British ships left Lynnhaven Bay and anchored in Hampton Roads, where they could more easily attack Norfolk. The following morning they sent out a tender and sounded the waters of the Elizabeth River channel, clearly signaling their intent to move up to the town. The British commander sent in a note complaining of the "extremely hostile" behavior of the citizenry and threatened to stop all traffic in and out of Chesapeake Bay. "You must be perfectly aware that the British flag never has, nor will be insulted with impunity," he warned. His squadron "could easily obstruct the whole trade of the Chesapeake."

His threat was far from idle. On July 8 a Norfolk pilot told Decatur he had overheard the first lieutenant of the *Bellona* say that his ship, as well as the *Leopard* and the *Melampus,* had all been lightened "for the purpose of lessening her Draft as much as possible" in order that they might sail up the Elizabeth River to Norfolk.

In preparation for the British attack Decatur, whose command now included the whole defense of Norfolk, moved the *Chesapeake* and the *Cybelle* to the narrows between Norfolk harbor and the channel, and placed four gunboats between them. If the British meant to carry out their threats, they would find the American reaction considerably more stubborn than it had been off Cape Henry.

By the middle of July the crisis had abated. The British squadron commander sailed for Halifax in the *Bellona,* carrying with him the four men who had been taken out of the *Chesapeake.* He was replaced by Captain Sir Thomas Masterman Hardy of the *Triumph.* Hardy had been Nelson's flag captain at Trafalgar, and was well known for his tact and diplomatic skills. He recognized the need to defuse a difficult situation and ordered the British squadron out of Chesapeake Bay. The ships would continue their blockade, but at sea, beyond sight of land, where their presence would not serve as a reminder of America's humiliation. He also sent the *Leopard* to Bermuda, never to return.

Late in July, three weeks after Decatur took command of the *Chesapeake,* two boatloads of Virginia militiamen, smartly decked out in their handsome uniforms and displaying colorful guidons and ensigns, passed the ship. They were pleased when the *Chesapeake*'s crew crowded onto the shrouds and cheered them, but were puzzled when there was no gun salute from the ship. The *Cybelle* had just paid them the signal honor of hoisting her national flag five times. Why could not the *Chesapeake* do as much? The answer turned out to be that by naval tradition, a vessel without honor could not confer honor on others. "We heard the explanation with a sigh," wrote a militia officer, "but immediately exclaimed 'if Barron has disgraced you, Decatur will retrieve your honor.'"

By late August, Decatur could write to Secretary Smith that "the *Chesapeake* is now in high order and the crew as well acquainted with the use of their guns as I could wish them. In fact, sir, I would rejoice in an opportunity, of risking my reputation in her alongside of one of their proudest ships of equal force. I feel confident, sir, if put to trial, the events would prove me not a vain boaster."

An official court of inquiry into the affair of the *Leopard* took place on board the *Chesapeake* in October. The court should have been convened at a much earlier date, but Barron had been ill for much of the summer. His health was always delicate—a considerable handicap for a senior naval officer—and he was subject to regular bouts of nervous exhaustion, particularly during periods of stress. His inability to attend the court was the principal reason the hearings had been so long delayed, and as it was he only attended the first week of the proceedings. Most of the rest of the time he remained at home, while his cousin, Robert Barraud Taylor, a

Norfolk attorney and one of the most distinguished lawyers in Virginia, stood in for him.

The court was made up of three captains, Isaac Hull, Isaac Chauncey, and Alexander Murray, who served as president. As was standard practice in that era, Murray hired a civilian, Littleton Waller Tazewell, to act as judge advocate.

Although Decatur had no official role in the proceedings, he made it a point to attend every session and to pay close attention to the testimony.

The purpose of the hearing was "to enquire into the causes of the surrender of the Chesapeak, a Frigate of the United States, then under the command of James Barron Esq., a Captain in the Navy of the United States, to a British vessel of war called the Leopard." Entered into the record were Barron's sailing orders, his report to Secretary of the Navy Smith, the exchange of notes with the captain of the *Leopard,* records of those killed and wounded, damage reports on the frigate, and an extract from the frigate's log. Another important document was an appeal that had been signed by the disgusted junior officers of the *Chesapeake* directly after the attack demanding Barron's court-martial.

Day after day, witnesses to the events of June 22 paraded through the great cabin giving their accounts. There was testimony that Barron had shown great personal courage and had exposed himself to gunfire throughout the bombardment, but there were many witnesses who thought his behavior during the action was confused and irresolute, and in the instance of lowering the colors, cowardly. Master Commandant Charles Gordon, second in command, testified that a shaken and distraught Barron had come up to him immediately after the encounter and asked him point-blank, "Do, Gordon, tell me what you think of my conduct." Gordon had tried to put as good a face on it as possible. "This being a question which required of me an immediate charge of cowardice or the expression of something to alleviate his apparently agitated feelings, I thought myself justified to say, 'I think your conduct correct while in my presence,' not meaning by my reply that I approved of the two essential points of his conduct, by these I mean first not going to quarters in time, and secondly his hauling down the colours when I conceived we were ready to return the fire."

Perhaps the most damning testimony was that of Lieutenant William Allen, the officer who had run with a hot coal from the galley to fire the *Chesapeake*'s only shot. "I do believe that the surrender of the *Chesapeake* was principally owing to Commodore Barron's want of courage and want of conduct," he told the court bluntly.

The court agreed, and concluded that during the attack Barron had "manifested great indecision, and a disposition to negotiate rather than a determination bravely to defend his ship." In a covering letter to the secretary of the navy enclosing the record of the court, Captain Murray wrote a stinging summary of the board's findings, placing the entire onus on James Barron. "A ship of war so nobly equipped as the *Chesapeake* then was, should never be taken off her guard," Murray wrote. "Behold the reverse, after an attack of a few minutes he struck his colors without consulting a single officer, thereby disgracing the flag of the United States."

The board's negative findings, and the continued national distress relating to the incident, made it incumbent upon President Jefferson to order a general court-martial.

The attention of the entire nation would be riveted on the upcoming trial. While every citizen could share a fury at the British navy for having precipitated such an outrage, there was a growing recognition that the American navy had also behaved in a shameful manner, and the country needed someone to blame. Given the findings of the court of inquiry, it was evident to many where that blame would fall.

Decatur understood the gravity of the charges that would be brought against Barron. He knew that by navy regulations an officer found "pusillanimously calling for quarter" could be sentenced to death, even shot on his own quarterdeck, as the Royal Navy had executed Admiral Byng in 1756. Decatur was reluctant to be part of such a decision, and when the secretary of the navy ordered him to serve on the court, he immediately tried to beg off. "I cannot in justice to Commodore Barron and my own feelings sit on this court without stating to you my opinion of the case," he wrote Smith on December 17.

> *When the unfortunate affair of the 22nd of June occurred, I formed an opinion that Commodore Barron had not done his duty; during the Court of Enquiry, I was present when the evidence of the officers was given in. I have since seen the opinion of the court, which opinion I think lenient. — It is probable that I am prejudiced against Commo. Barron and view his conduct in this case with more severity than it deserves; previous to her sailing, my opinion of him as a soldier was not favorable. Although, sir, I hope and trust I should most conscientiously decide on Commodore Barron's case, still, sir, there is no circumstance that would occasion me so much regret as to be compelled to serve on the court-martial that tries him. I have, therefore, to solicit that I may be excused from this duty.*

My opinion of him as a soldier was not favorable. The older man may have been an outstanding seaman, Decatur made clear, but he was no warrior. Here was the essential point of difference between Barron and Decatur. It was a difference that would embitter Barron. It would kill Decatur.

The secretary of the navy was quick to reject Decatur's request. In his December 26 answer to Decatur, he acknowledged his arguments but refused to release him from the court. "It does you honor," he wrote, "but if I were to excuse you from being a member of the court-martial, I should not be able to form a court. Other applications have been made, to which I have given a similar answer. I have every confidence in your honor and judgment as well as in the honor and judgment of others who have applied, and have no doubt you will do justice to the accused and to the country. I cannot, therefore, excuse any of you. Already there are fewer captains on the court than I could have wished."

A great deal was riding on the trial. Commodore James Barron was one of the most senior officers in the navy, and his court-martial would be one of the most important in the nation's short history, defining responsibilities and establishing important precedents. The whole country would be watching and the proceedings had to be seen as evenhanded. It was imperative that as far as practicable, Barron be judged by his peers. There were a total of only thirteen captains in the navy. One of them was Barron's brother Samuel, who was obviously ineligible. Three others had already served on the court of inquiry and could not be brought back for legal reasons. Of the remaining nine, four were unavailable. Decatur, already present in Norfolk, would have to serve.

Decatur made one last effort to get himself excused from the court. He sent copies of his correspondence with the secretary to Barron's counsel, in hopes that he would protest his presence on the court on legal grounds. Barron was apparently eager to make such a challenge, but was dissuaded by his lawyer—the same Robert Barraud Taylor who had defended him in the court of inquiry—who thought such a challenge might prejudice the entire court.

The trial opened on January 4, 1808, and once again was held in the great cabin of the *Chesapeake*. There were four defendants, who would be tried one after the other: Commodore James Barron, Master Commandant Charles Gordon, Captain John Hall of the marines, and the ship's gunner, William Hook. By far the most important of these was Barron, who would be tried first, on four charges: "for negligently performing the duty assigned him" (specifically, for his failure to properly inspect the *Chesapeake* while she was preparing for sea); "for neglecting on the probability of an engagement to clear his ship for action"; "for failing to encourage in his own person, his inferior officers and men, to fight courageously"; and for "not doing his utmost to take or destroy the *Leopard*, which vessel it was his duty to encounter."

Almost all the evidence brought forth in the court of inquiry was reintroduced in the court-martial, but this time it was presented in much
greater detail, for the court was seeking to find out not simply what had
happened, but who was responsible.

Everyone in the courtroom knew Decatur's opinion of Barron's role in
the action. He had not been shy about asserting blame after the court of
inquiry. But neither Decatur nor the other members of the court had
heard Barron's defense of his actions, and on February 3, the twenty-
seventh day of the trial, the judge advocate rested his case, and it was time
to hear Commodore Barron's version of the tumultuous events that had
occupied the court for so long.

Barron chose not to call any witnesses and asked that his lawyer be
allowed to read his defense to the court. The request was granted, and Mr.
Taylor then read aloud a long, detailed, and occasionally flowery defense,
written in the first person. Undoubtedly much of it was written by the
lawyer himself. The act of reading it must have been a considerable chore,
both for Mr. Taylor and the members of the court, who had to pay close
attention. It was a document of almost twenty-five thousand words, and
would have taken at least six hours to deliver. The record indicates that
the entire document was presented in a single sitting.

Barron opened his defense by claiming that for six months he had been
"the silent victim of misrepresentation and misconception; I shall have this
day an opportunity of vindicating my honour before an intelligent and
impartial tribunal." He moved on quickly to denying his responsibility for
the woeful condition of the *Chesapeake* when she set sail, pointing out that
he was not her captain, and citing navy regulations to place the onus on
Gordon. "It cannot be denied that these regulations consider captain Gordon as 'responsible for the whole conduct and good government of the
ship.' It was *his* duty 'to repair on board,' on *him* was the obligation of 'sta-
tioning and mustering the crew,' and regulating all the internal operations

of the ship, so as to have her 'constantly prepared for immediate action.'
Yet it is imputed to me as a crime, that I have not performed these duties,
thus expressly imposed on another officer."

A little later, he implicated the secretary of the navy, claiming that if he
had any inkling of potential hostile plans on the part of the British, he
should have made reference to them in his sailing orders to Barron, which
was not the case.

Eventually Barron moved from denial of his responsibility to an attack
on those who testified against him, particularly Gordon, who, he pointed
out, was motivated by self-interest. "The web of his destiny is interwoven
with mine. My condemnation is the pledge of his acquittal. If it be not
proved that the catastrophe resulted from my misconduct, the charge will
inevitably revert to that officer, from whose neglect of previous discipline
and arrangement, the surrender flowed."

He ridiculed the repeated charges of equivocation and cowardice from
his accusers, such as Lieutenant Allen, which he characterized as biased
and self-serving. "Great God! is the honour of an officer to be blasted by
such evidence?"

On the most emotionally touchy issue, that of striking the colors, Barron accepted full responsibility. This was a uniquely sensitive subject in
that particular court. Everyone in the room was aware that one of Barron's judges, Captain William Bainbridge, had on three different occasions been forced to order the flag lowered on his ships. Everyone in the
room was also aware that both Barron and Decatur had sat on the court
that cleared Bainbridge of any blame for the most recent occasion, when
he surrendered the *Philadelphia* to the Tripolitanians.

The presence of Bainbridge on the court may have encouraged Barron
to justify his order to strike in particularly forceful terms. "The wisest and
bravest men have yielded, without dishonour," he stated significantly. "My
conduct will I hope be tested by the honourable rules of real life, and not
by the visionary standard of speculative quixotism." But he immediately
followed this justification with a curious claim based on the relative
strength of the two ships: "It is admitted that the *Leopard* was a two decked

ship of more than fifty guns, of very superior weight to the *Chesapeake;* the *Chesapeake* a single decked ship, mounted 40 guns. The naval annals of the world, furnish no instance of a capture made by the smaller ship in such a conflict."

Such a bald assertion must have made Decatur bristle. The claim was self-serving and palpably false. What was Barron getting at? Every man on the court knew of and admired Lord Cochrane's legendary capture of the thirty-two-gun *El Gamo* by his doughty brig *Speedy,* of just fourteen guns, in 1800. And such lopsided victories were not confined to the Royal Navy. Even the little American navy had its examples of the triumph of zeal over iron. What of Trippe's gallant victory in the hand-to-hand combat with the Tripolitanian gunboats, when he and ten others conquered over odds of greater than three to one? Or, for that matter, what of Decatur's own little four-gun *Intrepid,* capturing and destroying the *Philadelphia?* And yet, there was Barron's (or his lawyer's) assertion, *"The naval annals of the world, furnish no instance of a capture made by the smaller ship in such a conflict."*

It was one of the defining moments of the trial.

On February 8, 1808, the court rendered its decision. Barron was found guilty, but due to mitigating circumstances he was neither sentenced to death nor permanently dismissed from the service. Instead, the court sentenced him "to be suspended from all command in the Navy of the United States, and that without Pay or official emoluments of any kind, for the period and term of five years."

Barron, who was convinced of his own innocence, was shocked at the severity of the sentence, and left the court deeply embittered. Decatur considered the sentence lenient.

TEN

Atlantic Tensions

Americans had been enraged by the *Leopard*'s attack on the *Chesapeake*, but it was hardly an isolated incident. Britain was in desperate need of crews to man its huge fleet, and for years the Royal Navy had been kidnapping sailors out of American ships in order to man her own. They routinely claimed that the captured sailors were British subjects, and in some cases this was true (as with Jenkin Ratford), but such claims were never anything more than a convenient excuse, and most of the men they abducted were native-born Americans.

Usually the British targeted American merchant vessels, but when the occasion presented itself they felt free to attack United States naval vessels as well. In 1798, off Havana, a Royal Navy squadron surrounded the United States sloop of war *Baltimore* and brazenly sent over a boarding party, mustered her crew, and stole fifty-five men out of her. In 1804 the British frigate *Cambrian*, in total disregard for American territorial rights, sailed into New York harbor, boarded a merchant vessel that had recently arrived, and carried off several crewmen and passengers. In April 1806, HMS *Leander*, of fifty-two guns, hovering off the entrance to New York harbor, deliberately fired into a coasting vessel and killed an American citizen on board.

Such blatant acts of aggression were in addition to the far more common high seas kidnappings that had become so common they were recognized as a normal occupational hazard of life on board American vessels. According to William Lyman, American consul in London, there were, in the year 1807, at least fifteen thousand American seamen serving in the British navy. In a report to Secretary of State James Madison he wrote, "There is not at this time, I believe, a single ship of war in the British navy whose crew does not consist partly, and in some instances on distant stations, principally, of American seamen."

America's smoldering resentment at Britain's high-handed behavior manifested itself in a general belief that another war with Great Britain was all but inevitable. Congress, which was trying desperately to avoid such a war, passed an Embargo Act that prohibited all trade by sea with any foreign power. When the act proved disastrous for the shipping interests of New England, it was replaced two years later by the Non-intercourse Act, which was only marginally less devastating. Although well intentioned, both acts amounted to a self-proclaimed blockade of American ports by the American government, and the U.S. Navy, much to the distress of many of its officers, was ordered to enforce it.

In 1808 Stephen Decatur, with the *Chesapeake* as his flagship, was put in charge of a squadron patrolling the coast from Maine to Virginia, chasing down and stopping American merchant vessels and sending them back into port for adjudication if an inspection indicated any violation of the law. Distasteful as the duty might be, particularly for a glory hound like Decatur, the need to patrol America's own shores brought at least one positive shift in naval policy. Coastal sailing was no job for gunboats. It required the use of real ships, capable of operating in open water and in every kind of weather, and that meant that the politicians in Washington were forced to alter their plans for a bathtub fleet designed for harbor defense and return to the deployment of more traditional oceangoing warships.

For Decatur personally, the shift offered an ephemeral but highly satisfying lagniappe. Because he now led a squadron, with more than one ship under his command, he was entitled to wear the courtesy rank of commodore, and could hoist his broad pennant on the main of his flagship. It was a purely nominal honor, and came with no increase in pay or other emoluments, but it was a welcome bit of glamour, and carried with it a gratifying increase in prestige.

In 1809, because of the increased need for more traditional warships, Decatur was ordered to the Washington Navy Yard to supervise the repair and refitting of the forty-four-gun frigate *United States,* which had been in ordinary since 1801, and which would require major work before she would again be ready for sea. The command of such a ship was a distinct honor and mark of respect, and Decatur welcomed the opportunity to renew the close ties he had with the venerable frigate. He had participated in her construction and launching, and had served in her both as midshipman and as lieutenant.

The *United States,* along with her sisters, the *Constitution* and the *President*, were the premiere warships of the American fleet, all three of them rugged heavyweights, designed for speed but built with the scantlings and thick walls of a ship of the line. Some considered them frigates in name only. Years earlier, Admiral Horatio Nelson, studying the Yankee hybrids in the Mediterranean, had remarked, "I see trouble for Britain in those big frigates from across the sea."

Decatur already knew the *United States* intimately, but now that he was to command her he developed an even closer, very personal relationship with her. Throughout the winter and early spring of 1809, as the frigate was being readied for sea, he came down to the shipyard every morning to observe the shipwrights working on her, and to gain a fresh appreciation of the genius of her designer, Joshua Humphreys. Long before he built the *United States,* Humphreys had described his vision for an American frigate in a letter to Robert Morris, the minister of finance:

"As our navy for a considerable time will be inferior in numbers [to those of the European powers], we are to consider what size ships will be most formidable, and be an overmatch for those of an enemy," he wrote. In event of war, he argued, there were two kinds of enemy warships that an American captain must be prepared to encounter on the open seas, the first being a single-decked frigate built for speed and maneuverability, and the second a massive but slow double-decked seventy-four-gun ship of the line, built for strength and firepower. What kind of ships should

America build to face such enemies? Humphreys suggested an interesting compromise, in essence a super frigate, a ship that was somewhat smaller than the 74s, but built with the same sort of strength, and designed for speed. Like all frigates, Humphreys's would carry only a single deck of guns, but they would be bigger, more powerful guns, almost equal to those carried by the 74s.

This more powerful battery gave Humphreys's super frigates a distinct advantage over an ordinary European frigate, fair weather or foul. And if one of his super frigates encountered a ship of the line, the American captain would have two options, depending on the weather. If the two ships met in rough seas, the American frigate would have an equal chance of success in battle, because the 74 would not be able to open the ports of her lower gun deck for fear of being swamped and would be forced to fight with her upper gun deck alone. If the two ships met in fair weather, where the 74 could use both decks of guns, the speedier American frigate could escape combat entirely, to fight another day. In Humphreys's elegant phrasing, he proposed building "such frigates as in blowing weather would be an overmatch for double-deck ships, and in light winds to evade coming to actions." And as Decatur could attest, that was precisely what he had accomplished.

The *United States* and her two sisters were probably the most advanced warships ever built in the age of fighting sail, and by the time Decatur was ready to bring his ship down the Potomac to Hampton Roads, he had every confidence that he could fulfill the promise inherent in her design.

Coincident with taking command of the *United States,* Decatur instituted a simple new regulation on board his ship that was quickly recognized throughout the navy as a valuable means of keeping the peace. Decatur's ruling required all midshipmen under his command to pledge themselves to neither give nor accept a challenge to a duel without previously reporting their disputes to him, and allowing him the opportunity to find some means of resolving the argument and cooling their hot tempers. Decatur made it clear that his new rule was not designed to abolish dueling—he believed it had a place in military life—but to temporize its fearful consequences, and to limit the practice to only the most intractable disagreements. In time his scheme became known as the Decatur Plan and was adopted by most other ship's captains. Over the years it undoubtedly saved many lives.

In 1810, Decatur's sailing orders called for him to cruise in the *United States* between Cape Henry and Florida and to give protection to American merchantmen plying that coast. The secretary of the navy's pointed comments about potential enemies reflected the prevailing mood in Washington:

> *You, like every other patriotic American, have observed and deeply feel the injuries and insults heaped on our country . . . and you must also believe that . . . no opportunity will be lost of adding to the outrage to which we have for years been subjected. Amongst these stands most conspicuous the inhuman and dastardly attack on our frigate* Chesapeake—*an outrage which prostrated the flag of our country and has imposed on the American people cause of ceaseless mourning. That same spirit which originated and has refused atonement for this act of brutal injustice exists still with Britain, and . . . we have no reason to expect any regard for our rights. What has been perpetrated may again be attempted; it is therefore our duty to be prepared and determined at every hazard to vindicate the injured honor of our navy and revive the drooping spirits of the nation. Influenced by these considerations, it is expected that, while you conduct the force under your command constently with the principles of a strict and upright neutrality, you are to maintain and support at any risk and cost the dignity of your flag and that, offering yourself no unjustified aggression, you are to submit to none—not even a menace or threats from a force not materially your superior.*

Decatur's reply expressed the same spirit:

> *Your instructions . . . have infused new life into the officers. No new*
> *indignity will pass with impunity and, unless I am much deceived in*
> *the feelings of our officers and the state of our ships, there would be no*
> *mortification or humility mixed with the feelings of our countrymen,*
> *should a contest take place.*

By the time the *United States* was once again ready for sea, three years had passed since the *Leopard*'s attack on the *Chesapeake,* and both the British and American navies were on hair-trigger alert. Mistakes became inevitable, and actual pitched battles between the two, which the diplomats in Washington and London had difficulty patching over, occurred more than once. On May 1, 1811, the British frigate *Guerriere,* cruising off New York, repeated the *Leopard*'s insulting actions by boarding an American warship, the brig *Spitfire,* and impressing an American-born citizen. When word of the outrage reached Commodore John Rodgers, he immediately set out in the USS *President,* another of the super frigates, to avenge the insult. On May 16, off Cape Henry, his lookouts spotted a ship in the distance that Rodgers thought likely to be the offending frigate. It was night before the two ships closed within hailing distance, and when challenged, the British vessel immediately opened fire. The Americans returned fire, and broadsides were exchanged. It quickly became evident from the small number of guns in her broadside that the stranger could not be the *Guerriere,* and Rodgers ordered his gun crews to cease firing. The following morning revealed that the offending ship was in fact HMS *Little Belt,* a sixth rate of only twenty-two guns. She had lost eleven killed and twenty-one wounded in the action. The American public, far from being embarrassed by this lopsided contest, hailed Rodgers as a hero for his "victory."

Not long after the attack on the *Little Belt,* the strained relations between Britain and America took a totally unexpected turn and brought attention to a man whose activities had been largely ignored in the years since his court-martial and disgrace in 1808. Commodore James Barron, following his suspension from the navy, had sought to make a living in the merchant service and had been employed sporadically as master of a merchant brig. In 1811 a curious account of his activities surfaced in Washington in a letter from Pernambuco, Brazil. The letter, written by Lieutenant William Lewis, USN, to Charles Goldsborough, chief clerk of the Navy Department, contained a sensational report of a purported conversation between Barron and the local British consul in Pernambuco. If accurate, the report represented damning evidence of what could only be read as treasonous behavior on Barron's part:

> *I think it proper to communicate to you for the information of the Secretary of the Navy that Captain James Barron, while in this place, in a merchant brig from Norfolk, did say to a Mr. Lyon, British Consul at the time, and now residing here that even if the* Chesapeake *had been prepared for action, he would not have resisted the attack of the* Leopard; *assigning as a reason, that he knew (as did also our government) there were deserters on board his ship. He said to Mr. Lyon farther, that the president of the United States knew there were deserters on board, and of the intention of the British ships to take them, and that his ship was ordered out under these circumstances, with the view to bringing about a contest which might embroil the two nations in a war. He told Mr. Lyon that he had private letters in his possession from officers, high in the government, approving his conduct in the affair of the* Leopard. *I obtained this information from Mr. Thomas Goodwin of Baltimore (brother of Lieutenant Ridgley) who received it from Mr. Lyon himself; not in confidence but in company where a number of Americans were present. Mr. Lyon considers Barron as having been highly injured in the business.*
>
> *I always knew that Barron was a man of the most vindictive heart. He has no doubt, said these things with a view to revenge himself.*
>
> *I am now convinced that he is not only a coward but a traitor, for I can call by no other name a man who would talk in this way to an Englishman,—and an Englishman in office.*

The remarkable letter, so shocking in its disclosures but based entirely on hearsay, was discussed by the appropriate officials and then placed in the department files. It would eventually emerge again, years later, as one more element in the mosaic of incidents, disclosures, charges, and countercharges that would lead at last to the meeting at Bladensburg.

Toward the close of 1811, Decatur brought his ship into Norfolk for recoppering, and he and Susan returned to their home and resumed their accustomed place in the social life of the little city. He was still living at home a few months later when he became party to one of the truly remarkable coincidences in his career.

In February 1812, HMS *Macedonian,* a thirty-eight-gun frigate, sailed into the Chesapeake and dropped anchor in Hampton Roads. The arrival of a British warship was a rare event and created considerable excitement in Norfolk. As a direct response to the *Leopard* incident, the American government had closed its seaports to all British warships, and as a result, the locals had seen almost nothing of the Royal Navy for the past five years. The one exception to the ban were warships that might from time to time arrive on diplomatic business. The *Macedonian* turned out to be such a ship. Her captain, the aristocratic John Surman Carden, came ashore bearing large sealed packages for the British minister in Washington and was welcomed by Colonel Hamilton, the British consul, who made arrangements for their shipment. Carden had heard much about the strong anti-British feelings in America and was nervous that the presence of his ship might incite some angry reaction from the local citizenry. The consul laughed and assured him that his anxieties were overblown. When Carden told him he expected to remain in Virginia for at least a fortnight until the legation in Washington sent a return package to the *Macedonian,* Hamilton immediately began arranging entertainments for his visitors. The move was welcomed, especially among the naval personnel stationed in Norfolk. Because of the strained political situation, there had been very few opportunities for American naval officers to meet with their British peers, a fact they very much regretted. Americans might be outraged by British policies, but their anger did not extend to the Royal Navy, which they saw as responsible only for carrying out those policies. As professionals, American officers held the British navy in the highest regard, and they were confident enough to consider themselves the equal—in skill and daring, if not in size—to their British opposite numbers, and they hungered for opportunities for direct interaction with the undisputed rulers of the sea. High on Hamilton's guest list was Commodore Decatur, who, because of his exploits in Tripoli, was likely to be one of the few Americans that Carden might have heard of.

There is no record of how many times Decatur and Carden met during the Englishman's stay in Norfolk, but it is evident that there were a number of invitations exchanged, and that the two men grew quite close. Carden and his officers were regular guests at the Decatur table. On such occasions there was always considerable good-natured bantering between the officers concerning the parlous diplomatic situation between their two countries, and the prospect that they might soon find themselves at war with one another. But there was always time for serious naval discussion as well. At one such dinner Decatur brought up the matter of armament. He was proud of the power of his twenty-four-pounder long guns, and said as much. Carden, who was a somewhat older man, listened politely to his host and then dismissed his enthusiasm out of hand. He explained condescendingly that the Royal Navy had already tried twenty-four-pounders in their frigates, but had found the eighteen-pounders more efficient.

Eventually, when it came time for Carden to return to England, the two captains made the ritual reference to the possibility of meeting in the future as enemies, and Carden is reported to have remarked, "Though your ships may be good enough, and you are a clever set of fellows, what practice have you had in war? There's the rub. . . . Should we meet as enemies, what do you suppose will be the result?"

To which Decatur is said to have responded, "The conflict will undoubtedly be a severe one, for the flag of my country will never be struck while there is a hull for it to wave from."

While the somewhat overblown phrasing may be the invention of later writers, there is little question that such sentiments reflected the true feelings of both men.

A few months after Carden's departure, the war that the British and American officers had so blithely suggested, became a reality. In June 1812, an angry Congress, weary of the constant maritime humiliations inflicted by Britain, decided to take drastic action.

At the time, Britain had more than six hundred warships, including 124 ships of the line, each carrying 60 or more guns, and 116 frigates, carrying anywhere from 28 to 50 guns. America's total fleet consisted of three super frigates, rated at 44 guns, as well as three standard-sized frigates of 38 guns, three sloops of war of 32, 28, and 18 guns, and seven smaller vessels with around 12 guns each. Taken altogether, the American ships mounted fewer than 450 guns, against a British total of over 20,000. Despite this lopsided disparity Congress, propelled by an overweening hubris that is still difficult to comprehend, declared war on Great Britain.

ELEVEN

29° N × 29° 30′ W

At dawn on October 25, 1812, the USS *United States* was steering under easy sail toward the southwest, propelled by a stiff southeasterly breeze. The ship was sailing alone, having parted company with the *Argus* two weeks earlier, and was now somewhere between the Canaries and the Cape Verde Islands, off the coast of Africa. It was a sparkling clear morning, and high overhead in the tops lookouts combed the horizon for anything they might find in this seemingly limitless expanse of open sea.

Stephen Decatur was hunting for anything British—a rich Indiaman on her way home laden with the treasures of the East India Company would have been particularly welcome, or a merchantman outward bound to the Cape or the Caribbean. But Decatur and his men were eager for a fight, and a British man-of-war would have been equally welcome. They were cruising in well-traveled sea lanes, familiar to sailors since the days of the Roman Empire, but that was no guarantee they would find what they sought. The ocean was an infinitely larger place in the age of fighting sail, and the search for an enemy was unpredictable and often frustrating. Everyone on board knew that the likelihood of coming across another vessel was largely a matter of chance. Days, even weeks might go by without a sighting. But today would prove to be an exception.

Soon after sunrise, there was a call from overhead.

"Sail ahoy!"

"Where away?" the officer of the deck shouted back.

"To the south-southwest, broad off on the weather beam." Immediately, the larboard railing of the spar deck was alive with excited faces straining to catch a glimpse of the strange sail to the south. It took about ten minutes before the tiny, indecipherable speck, previously hidden by the curvature of the earth, became visible to those on deck.

Decatur studied the stranger through his glass. She was still too far away for him to make out any details, but she was sailing with the wind, and therefore approaching rapidly. In another hour he might be able to get some idea of her size, and what kind of ship she was.

He passed the word to his sailing master to alter course to meet her. Decatur, never more than an indifferent sailor himself, was happy to leave the handling of his ship to others. He would decide where she should go, and someone else could figure out how to get her there. Decatur could then concentrate on what to do with her once she arrived. The sailing master shouted a few quick orders to the topmen, and almost immediately a great cloud of fresh canvas caught the wind and pushed the ship forward toward the stranger.

Was she a friend? Not likely in these latitudes. Neutral? Always possible. Foe? Very likely. Britannia did, after all, rule the waves. Her ships were everywhere, but in an age when sailing under false colors was the rule rather than the exception, and the identity of a ship was never easy to ascertain, it would take time to make sure. Whatever the answer, the men in the *United States* were confident they could outfight anything they could not outrun.

It was still far too early to send the crew to battle stations, but from the quarterdeck Decatur could see that a number of men had already collected around the carronades. He had great confidence in his crew and knew most of them by name. Many had served with him for years, since he took command of the *Chesapeake* in 1807, or even earlier, in the Barbary Wars. They were "followers," loyal to the captain they loved and trusted, men who had quite literally dedicated their lives to him.

Descending to the gun deck, he saw men gathered together by the twenty-four-pounders that lined the entire length of either side of the ship. Like all wooden warships, the *United States* carried more guns than her rating indicated. Although rated as a 44, she in fact carried fifty-five guns in all, including howitzers in the tops.

Eventually, the stranger's hull rose over the horizon, which meant she was now some seven or eight miles distant. Even without a telescope, the sharp-eyed members of the crew could see that she carried three masts. If she was a warship, she was most likely either a frigate or a ship of the line.

It was time to clear the ship for action. Decatur gave the order to beat to quarters, and the ship's drummer, who had been standing by expectantly, sounded the familiar tattoo. Immediately, the ship's well-drilled crew ran through the familiar routine of opening the ports, casting loose the guns, and running them out. There was no need to load, for the guns were already double-shotted. The powder monkeys were sent below to fetch powder horns, extra cartridges, and slow match from the magazines.

Everything went like clockwork. Bulkheads were knocked away. Hand weapons—cutlasses and boarding pikes and buckets of pistols, all loaded and primed—were stacked around the masts in preparation for hand-to-hand fighting. Tubs of sand were placed in convenient locations, to prevent slipping on the deck. Marines went into the tops, to provide musket fire, and "trimmers" to handle the sails.

It was 8:30 in the morning.

The stranger had by now drawn close enough for Decatur and his officers to clearly make out the guns protruding from her sides. She was indeed a man-of-war, which meant she was almost certainly British. When the news was announced to the people, a wave of excitement ran through the ship. Even with the glass it was still difficult to make out whether the stranger carried one or two gun decks. Like everyone else on board, Decatur hoped she was a frigate, but until he knew the nature of the warship he was approaching, he could make no final plans. Decatur was willing to take chances, but he was never a fool. He ordered his sailing master to wear, in order to gain the weather gauge. Placing his ship upwind of the stranger would allow him to control the action and even to escape, should the enemy vessel prove too large to fight.

Of course there was always the possibility that there would be no fight. For all her bristling guns, the stranger might turn out to be French, or Swedish, or to belong to some other navy with which America had no quarrel. But Decatur, and virtually everyone on board his ship, wanted the stranger to be British. Most of them, probably a majority, had served in the *Chesapeake,* and they had been waiting five years to avenge the *Leopard*'s attack.

While the two ships continued to close, one of the powder monkeys, a ten-year-old boy named Jack Creamer, approached Decatur and after knuckling his forehead respectfully, said, "I wish my name to be put down on the roll, sir." The boys, although members of the crew, were never officially recruited, and were therefore not subject to all the regulations. "Why so?" asked Decatur. "So I may have a share of the prize money," Jack replied. Decatur laughed and promised to take care of the matter.

Decatur had much to think about. Two months earlier, at the end of August, he had witnessed a scene of wild celebration in Boston when a triumphant Isaac Hull had returned to port in the *Constitution* with the stunning news that he had captured and sunk the British frigate *Guerriere.* It was an astonishing victory. In the preceding twenty years of almost incessant naval warfare between Britain and France the two great sea powers had fought innumerable single-ship actions, but only once had the French triumphed, in 1805 when the *Milan* captured the *Cleopatra.* On every other occasion, the British had beaten the French. Now in the opening weeks of America's new war, Isaac Hull had drawn first blood against the proudest, most powerful naval force in history! The streets of Boston were decked with flags, and citizens crowded the streets and housetops to cheer the new heroes. Decatur was as thrilled as everyone else, and was unstinting in his congratulations for his old shipmate's great victory. But for all his genuine delight in Hull's achievement, Decatur was by nature competitive. Hull's victory could not but spark a desire on his part to at least equal, and if possible surpass, that great triumph. Now, as he watched the approaching stranger, he wondered if she might provide the opportunity for which he longed.

As Decatur's ship wore to starboard in an attempt to gain the weather gauge, the stranger anticipated the move and hauled up, thwarting the American and forcing Decatur to wear again, this time to larboard.

But while the stranger had skillfully protected a tactical advantage, her move revealed an important fact—she had only a single gun deck. She was a frigate after all, but of whose navy? Moments later in answer the stranger ran up a huge Union Jack. She was indeed British, and that meant there would be a fight. A great cheer broke out on the ship. Decatur ordered the American colors displayed, and there was another shout when the Stars and Stripes unfurled overhead, snapping briskly from each mast. Doubtless, there was an equivalent burst of enthusiasm on the British ship. These men lived to fight.

By now the two ships were running side by side in the same direction on a parallel course toward the morning sun, separated by perhaps a mile of open sea. Decatur wanted a sense of the range, and ordered a broadside. Moments later, there was a ragged paroxysm of thunder as one after another of the guns fired, making the decks jump and sending up a white cloud of smoke that all but obscured the British ship. Leaning through the smoke, Decatur could just make out the splashes as the shots fell short— but not by much. Those had been double-shotted guns. With single rounds, he knew he could now reach the enemy every time, and gave the order to fire at will.

William Henry Allen, Decatur's first lieutenant, broke into a broad grin as he relayed the order. Allen was the man who had fired the only shot from the *Chesapeake* back in 1807. He had spent years exercising the crew of the *United States* in anticipation of this day. Every night, he and the other officers had spent endless hours discussing the pros and cons of various theories of naval warfare. How you mixed your shot made all the difference: grape and canister to scatter the enemy, chain and langrage to cut up the sails and rigging, solid shot to hole the hull and wound or carry away the masts. Allen knew precisely how he wanted to fight the guns. He and Decatur had long since determined that the most efficient tactic was to concentrate first on the sails and rigging. Take away a ship's ability to maneuver, and she would be helpless to fight back.

The battle was joined, and both ships now opened fire in earnest. Decatur stood on the quarterdeck where he could not see his twenty-four-pounders below on the gun deck, but he could hear and feel them, and he liked the noise they made, and the shocks they sent through the ship. They were firing at such a rapid rate that it was difficult to see through the thick smoke, which clung to the ship's rigging, even as she pushed rapidly through the sea. Lieutenant Allen had trained his gun crews well. It is quite likely that on that day they demonstrated a speed and degree of proficiency unmatched on any other ship in the world.

The secondary battery on the spar deck, made up of short-range carronades, was quite useless at the distance that still separated the two ships. Later, when the ships closed, the forty-two-pound shot fired by the squat little carronades could prove decisive, but for the present Decatur was content to let their crews stand idle, while the battle continued at long range.

Sea battles were by their nature always fraught with risk and unexpected perils, but Decatur was not overly concerned. He held all the advantages. He had a larger, more strongly built ship than the British, with more guns, larger guns, more powerful guns. His main concern was not whether he could win the battle—he was confident enough on that point—but whether he could win it in the way he wanted.

The concentrated fire on the stranger's masts began to tell. The British frigate's mizzen top was the first to go, falling forward into her main top, tangling her sails and rigging. One of the American gunners shouted, "We've made a brig of her!" Decatur, who was standing close enough to hear, shouted back, "Aim at the mainmast, and she'll be a sloop!" Soon enough, a combination of American shots did just that. The mainmast came crashing down into the fore topmast, and the enemy ship was reduced to little more than a hulk. The stubby remains of her three masts now held only two bits of sail—a ripped and fluttering foresail, clewed up awkwardly, and an almost useless forestay. For all intents and purposes she was dead in the water, and at the mercy of the Americans.

But still she fought on.

The ships had been moving closer to each other throughout the action, and were now well within range of the carronades. Decatur gave the order for them to commence firing, which effectively doubled the weight of metal the Americans could now send into the enemy ship. The American fire became overwhelming. By traditional practice, it only remained now for the Americans to bring their ship alongside the enemy and board her, to capture her in hand-to-hand fighting.

But Decatur had a radically different endgame strategy in mind. He had held the advantage from the beginning, and his ship had suffered only minimal damage and casualties. Without explanation, he ordered his gun crews to cease firing, and turning to his sailing master, told him to pull the ship away from the action. To the utter surprise and mystification of the British, the American ship filled her mizzen topsail and shot ahead, crossing the British ship's highly vulnerable and unprotected bow. Decatur was now in a perfect position to sink the enemy, but instead of firing, he simply moved off, leaving the mystified British to wonder. At first they thought the totally unprecedented American behavior could only mean that the Yankee ship had spotted a British squadron on the horizon and was trying to get away before its arrival. But when the American ship had moved about two miles distant, she hove to. Clearly she was not trying to escape from anyone. There had to be another explanation, but what it might be remained a puzzle to the exhausted but defiant British.

Decatur explained his highly unorthodox maneuver to his officers. It was simple enough. The British were beaten, but they were so busy being brave that they had not noticed they had lost. Decatur simply wanted to give them sufficient time to recognize that their only option was surrender. An hour later, the Americans wore ship and returned. The British had spent the time cutting away the wreckage from the upper parts of the ship, but she remained as helpless as before. The American ship ranged up to a raking position, with long guns and carronades run out, ready to send the British to the bottom. Further resistance was now pointless, but would the stubborn British recognize the obvious? At last, to Decatur's relief, the helpless enemy lowered her colors.

From the quarterdeck, Decatur, using a speaking trumpet asked the enemy ship to identify herself.

"His Majesty's ship *Macedonian,*" came the answer, "Captain John S. Carden."

One of the first Americans to arrive on board the *Macedonian* was shocked by the shambles he encountered. "Fragments of the dead were distributed in every direction," he wrote, "the decks covered with blood, one continued agonizing yell of the unhappy wounded; a scene so horrible of my fellow-creatures, I assure you, deprived me very much of the pleasure of victory."

A disoriented Captain Carden, still in a state of shock, but dressed in his most presentable uniform, was rowed over to the *United States,* where Decatur greeted him warmly. The Englishman did not at first recognize him. He ceremoniously handed over his sword in token of surrender, but Decatur waved it away. "Sir, I cannot receive the sword of a man who has so bravely defended the honor of it."

Decatur reintroduced himself and reminded Carden of their previous meetings in Norfolk. Carden, still caught up in the crisis of battle, only slowly regained his composure.

"I am an undone man," he said with dignity, straining to mask his mortification. "I am the first British naval officer who has struck his flag to an American."

Decatur was quick to bring him up to date. "May I inform you sir, you are mistaken. Your *Guerriere* has been taken." When Carden seemed not to understand, Decatur explained gently, "The flag of a British frigate was struck before yours." Carden looked at Decatur as if he were mad.

TWELVE

"Of Equal Force"

The battle was over, but there was still another contest to be fought, another victory to be won. Even as his ship's guns were cooling, Decatur had started planning his next steps, the first of which was to somehow salvage the *Macedonian,* to keep her from sinking, and bring her home. He was convinced that Isaac Hull had made a serious mistake when, after capturing the *Guerriere,* he chose to put her to the torch and blow her up. Decatur understood the American public, and foresaw the powerful effect it would have on his fellow citizens if he could bring a captured British warship home for all to see, and he was determined to do so if at all possible.

His second goal, closely related to the first but requiring a totally different strategy, was to wrest the maximum prize money from his capture. Decatur had a score to settle. His destruction of the *Philadelphia* had been recognized the world over as a triumph of naval daring, but Congress had celebrated it on the cheap, authorizing only a few commemorative baubles and denying Decatur and his men any award of prize money. The slight had been a matter of deep humiliation. He was chagrined that his influence in Washington had not been sufficient to win prize money for his men, every one of whom had risked his life on a mission of extreme danger.

As soon after the British surrender as practicable, Decatur sent Lieutenant Allen and the ship's carpenters over to inspect the *Macedonian* and see if she could be made sufficiently seaworthy to withstand a twenty-two-hundred-mile journey across the Atlantic in early winter. The voyage was likely to be difficult, and the ship would undoubtedly require considerable

work. Allen found her to be in parlous shape. She was leaking danger-
ously, with almost a hundred holes in her hull, many below the waterline,
and her masts and rigging a total wreck, but he returned with a cautiously
optimistic report and Decatur immediately appointed him prizemaster,
with orders to effect all necessary repairs.

The work on the *Macedonian,* carried out by a mixed crew of American
and English sailors, took almost a week. During that time the two ships
remained hove to in the middle of busy sea lanes, where the chance of dis-
covery by British naval forces remained a constant threat. But Decatur's
luck held. By October 30, five days after the battle, Lieutenant Allen had
succeeded in rigging a jury mizzenmast and thereby converting the *Macedonian* into a bark. That was good enough for Decatur. He was understandably anxious about remaining in such an exposed location, and he
gave the order to forgo any further repairs and get the two ships home as
quickly as possible. The slow and difficult journey, through waters
infested with Royal Navy ships, took a little over a month, during which
time they encountered not one enemy vessel. But the seas were not
entirely empty. They spoke a Swedish merchantman bound for Cadiz,
and Decatur arranged for her to take Captain Carden's report of the battle
to Europe, so that the news of the capture of the *Macedonian* might reach
the Admiralty in an expeditious manner. He was just as interested in getting the word to England as he was to get it to his own people.

The letter that Carden sent off to the Admiralty must have been a particularly painful one to write: "It is with the deepest regret I have to acquaint
you for the information of my Lords Commissioners of the Admiralty
that His Majesty's late Ship *Macedonian* was captured on the 25th Instant
by the U.S. Ship *United States,* Commodore Decatur Commander, the
details as follows. . . ."

He went on to describe the action in a straightforward manner, until
the terrible climax, when his ship "being a perfect wreck and an unman-
ageable log," he had been forced to surrender. He gave the grim details of

casualties. "I am sorry to say our loss is very severe. I find by this days muster, thirty six killed, three of whom linger'd a short time after the Battle, thirty six severely wounded, many of whom cannot recover, and thirty two slight wounds, who may all do well, total one hundred and four." Carden neglected to mention the equally painful fact that the total American casualties amounted to only seven killed and five wounded, barely more than 10 percent of the British losses.

Toward the close of Carden's report, the tone shifted and became somewhat disingenuous and self-serving. The same man who had so airily dismissed Decatur's faith in his twenty-four-pounders when the two men discussed their ships in Norfolk earlier in the year now described the USS *United States* in such a way as to imply that the fight had been somehow unfair. "On being taken onboard the Enemys Ship, I ceased to wonder at the result of the Battle; the United States is built with the scantline of a seventy four gun Ship, mounting thirty long twenty four pounders (English Ship Guns) on her Main Deck, and twenty two forty two pounders, Carronades, with two long twenty four pounders on her Quarterdeck and Forecastle. Howitzer Guns in her Tops, and a travelling Carronade on her upper Deck, with a Complement of four Hundred and seventy eight pick'd men."

Around the same time that Captain Carden was composing his letter to the Admiralty, Decatur was working up his own version of the action in a report addressed to the secretary of the navy. While it closely parallels Carden's account in terms of the basic details of the battle, Decatur's comparison of the two vessels differs substantially from the British version. While Carden emphasized the significant differences between the two ships in terms of size and armament, Decatur made a point of their similarities: "Sir, I have the honour to inform you that on the 25th Inst. being in the Lat. 29 N. Long. 29° 30 W., We fell in with, & after an action of an hour & a half, captured His Britannic Majesty's ship *Macedonian* commanded by Captain John Carden, and mounting 49 carriage guns. . . . She is a frigate of the largest class—two years old—four month out of dock, and reputed one of the best sailers in the British service."

It was true enough that most Royal Navy frigates were indeed smaller than the *Macedonian,* but Decatur was gilding the lily to describe her as "a frigate of the largest class." He was quick to recognize that the best means of blurring the difference between the two ships lay in carefully doctoring the definition of their armament.

It was accurate to point out that the *Macedonian,* although rated as a thirty-eight-gun ship, actually carried forty-nine, just as Decatur's own *United States,* rated a 44, actually carried fifty-five. But Decatur, in his report and in the months of negotiation to come, would unfailingly define the *Macedonian* as a forty-nine-gun ship, and the *United States* as a 44, with the clear implication that the *Macedonian,* with its five "extra" guns, was the more heavily armed vessel, and by extension, the more powerful, which was a significant distortion of fact. When it came to special pleading, Decatur was every bit the equal of Carden.

The reason for Decatur's deliberate obfuscation lay in the law governing the awarding of prize money, which stated that if an American ship captured an enemy vessel "of equal or superior force," the entire value of the capture was to be divided among the officers and men of the victorious ship. If, however, the enemy vessel was of lesser force, the American captor was to receive only a "moiety," that is, one-half of the value.

Decatur was laying the groundwork for a large award of prize money, perhaps a very large award. The years since the war with Tripoli had taught him just how unreliable were the promises of politicians. If he wanted something, it was best not to trust others to get it for him. In the weeks to come, he would take care of things himself, and in the process he would repeatedly insist, against all arguments to the contrary, that the 1,082-ton *Macedonian* with its eighteen-pounder battery was just as large and powerful as the 1,579-ton *United States* with its twenty-four-pounders. It was nonsense, of course, but it was the only way that he and those who served under him would get what had rightfully been owed them for eight years.

From the moment Decatur arrived in Connecticut on December 4 with the glorious news of his newest conquest, he proved himself as formidable a master of self-promotion and manipulator of public sentiment as he was a naval leader.

He began his campaign within hours of his arrival, when, on landing at New London, he learned that a great naval ball was to be given in Washington in honor of Isaac Hull and the officers of the *Constitution*. The celebration was scheduled for four days hence, and if he hurried, he was told, he could get to Washington in time to attend. But Decatur deliberately chose not to go. His presence would indeed have caused a sensation, but he did not wish to steal his fellow officers' thunder. He might need their good will in the weeks to come to help press his case with the prize court. Instead, he chose to send one of his junior lieutenants, Archibald Hamilton, to announce the victory. Lieutenant Hamilton happened to be the son of Secretary of the Navy Paul Hamilton, and Decatur was going to need the secretary's goodwill as well. What better way to ingratiate himself with such an important minister than to give his son the honor of proclaiming such a gratifying message to the nation's leaders? Young Hamilton started immediately for Washington, carrying with him the *Macedonian*'s battle flag along with Decatur's judiciously phrased report of the action, with its suggestion that the British frigate was at least of equal, if not superior strength.

As Decatur knew would be the case, young Hamilton's arrival at the ball, the dust of the road still on his uniform, and his dramatic presentation of the *Macedonian*'s colors to Dolley Madison, the president's wife, in front of the cream of Washington's society, triggered a welling up of patriotic euphoria that would be talked about for years to come. The very absence of Decatur at this moment of historic significance was perceived as an instance of noble modesty that lent additional stature to his already heroic public persona.

It was also no accident that only days after the ball, in the pages of the influential *Niles' Weekly Register,* an interview with an unnamed naval officer (almost certainly Lieutenant Hamilton) openly acknowledged the disparity in size between the two ships, but put forth a curious rationalization of their relative strengths:

> *An officer of the frigate United States, speaking of Decatur's late victory, says—"I am aware it will be said, that she is a little ship, with five guns less than you, and a hundred men less, and carries lighter metal &c.—well, all this is true—she is inferior in all these—but she is just such a ship as the English have achieved all their single ship victories in—twas in such a ship that SIR ROBERT BARLOW took the Africaine—that SIR MICHAEL SEYMOUR took the Brune, and afterwards the Nieman—that capt. MILNE took the Vengeance, capt. COOK the La Forte, capt. LAVIE the Guerriere, capt. ROWLEY the Venus, and God knows how many others; she is, in tonnage, men and guns, such a ship as the English prefer to all others."*

In other words, the *Macedonian* was indeed statistically inferior to the *United States,* but since that was the way the British chose to fight, the battle was therefore between equals.

Decatur wrote Secretary Hamilton that he was anxious to move quickly on the matter of prize money so that his crew might receive the cash before they sailed off again. The secretary was only too happy to oblige, and on December 29, he let Decatur know the matter was already well in hand.

> *With respect to the prize, two points namely, her relative force & her value must be immediately ascertained. This can best be done by the appointment of referees on the part of the Department. I nominate Jacob Lewis Esqr now at New York as one of the referees. You will be pleased to appoint another & should the two so appointed disagree, they will choose a third whose decision shall be conclusive.*

The objects to be particularly attended to by the referees are 1. the rel-
ative force of the two frigates, the United States *and the* Macedonian
including her rigging, apparel, armaments & everything belonging to
her—at such valuation the Navy Depmt will purchase her & put her
in commission. Should She be considered equal in force to the United
States, the Department will pay to the Captors the whole amount of her
valuation—if of inferior force, one moiety only unless Congress should
vote the whole to the captors.

The fix was in.

Decatur could not have asked for a more obliging candidate to represent
the navy's interests than Secretary Hamilton's choice of Commander Jacob
Lewis. He was an officer much junior to Decatur, and unlikely to make trouble for his gallant and revered superior. To represent his own side, Decatur
selected Dr. John Bullus, a close friend and prominent figure in naval affairs.
By the time the judges were appointed the *Macedonian* lay at anchor in New
York harbor, and after a quick inspection the two representatives were able to
agree that despite significant differences in size, battery, and construction, the
two ships, *mirabile dictu,* were of equal force. To further justify such a judgment, they brought in a third party to help them determine the overall value
of the prize. They selected a prominent New York shipbuilder, Henry Eckford, who was unwilling to support the finding that the two ships were of
equal force, but was quite happy to endorse the less controversial finding that
the total value of the *Macedonian* was two hundred thousand dollars:

We the undersigned, having been appointed referees, Jacob Lewis on
the part of the Naval Department, & John Bullus on behalf of the
Captors, to decide the relative force of the Frigates United States and
Macedonian, have, after a strict and careful survey, decided as fol-
lows—That the Frigate Macedonian upon general Naval calculations
is of equal force to the Frigate United States, and that the Hull, Spars
& Rigging, together with her military armament, ammunition, Three
months stores & Provisions are worth Two hundred thousand,—We

have further to remark that a difference of opinion to the value having arisen, a third person was called in, Mr. Eckford, an eminent Naval Constructor, whose signature is annexed to this decision. /s/ J. Lewis, John Bullus, Henry Eckford.

The decision was rushed to William Jones, the new secretary of the navy, who was just as willing to cooperate with Decatur as his predecessor, and who immediately wrote to him, declaring that the navy was now ready to pay on the barrelhead:

I have received . . . the decision of the Referees, as to the relative force and value of the frigate Macedonian, *which gives to the captors the whole of that vessel — and values her at Two Hundred thousand dollars — It now only remains for you to name the agents to whom you wish this sum to be paid, in order that it may be immediately paid over & distributed according to Law.*

The scheme had worked. Decatur, through a careful handling of details, and with the tacit cooperation of two different secretaries of the navy, had arranged for the U.S. government to publicly acknowledge that black was white, that up was down, that the sun rose in the west and sank in the east, and that the *Macedonian* and the *United States* were of equal force. He named his father-in-law, Luke Wheeler, and his lawyer, Littleton Waller Tazewell, as his agents.

And then at the last moment, on the very day that Luke Wheeler arrived at the Navy Department to arrange for the transfer of the full two hundred thousand dollars in gold, a new and unexpected obstacle suddenly arose from out of nowhere and threatened to bring down the whole elaborately contrived rationalization.

The obstacle was a formidable one: namely, Secretary of the Treasury Albert Gallatin. Gallatin was a powerful figure in Washington, a Jeffersonian idealist who had spent years fighting against a strong military establishment—he had led the campaign for a gunboat navy—and he was convinced that huge awards of prize money were capricious, unfair, and therefore pernicious. Despite the decision of the prize court, he refused to authorize the payment of two hundred thousand dollars out of the public treasury. He was willing to compromise, he told the secretary of the navy, and would authorize the withdrawal of half that amount, but he refused to go along with the blatant fiction that the *Macedonian* was of equal force to the *United States*.

A distraught and very embarrassed William Jones laid out the problem to Luke Wheeler. He was still prepared to give Decatur and his men the full award, he explained weakly, but he did not see how he could do so without Gallatin's acquiescence.

Luke Wheeler was not to be so easily put off. He was made of sterner stuff than that, and knew how to meet a major challenge with the same coolness as his son-in-law. After considering the situation overnight, he returned to the offices of the naval secretary the next day and handed him a letter. While couched in polite enough terms, the letter contained a formidable threat that if carried out would shake the government to its foundations:

> *In response to the conversation I had the honor to hold with you yesterday respecting the prize money which is due to the Captors of the Frigate Macedonian, I hope I may be permitted further to remark, that . . . Commissioned officers, from a variety of considerations, cannot permit themselves to come into Collision with the Government, similar considerations however cannot be expected to influence the petty officers & Seamen of the Ship, whose Agents Mr Tazewell & myself likewise are, and it becomes our duty to urge their Rights with all due difference to the Government. I am persuaded Sir, that there is not a Court of Justice competent to the decision which would not decide the principle that a First Rate British frigate is, in all points of a National view, equal to a first rate Frigate of any other nation of the world.*

The threat was straightforward and clear. Stephen Decatur and his fellow officers might be too much the gentlemen to sue the U.S. government, but the petty officers and common sailors who served under them were under no such obligation. If they chose to bring their case to court, the American public would be invited to consider how—in the midst of a war—the foreign-born Albert Gallatin ("that damned Genevan," his enemies called him) had withheld prize money from the brave heroes who were defending their country. As Wheeler turned to leave, he told Jones he was free to show Gallatin the letter if he so chose.

Wheeler's threat worked. Faced with the prospect of a public outcry in favor of the nation's favorite hero, Gallatin was persuaded to withdraw his objections. The full two hundred thousand dollars was paid out to the men of the USS *United States*. Decatur's share came to thirty thousand dollars, a sum probably equivalent to over a half million present-day dollars. Jack Creamer, the ten-year-old boy who before the battle had requested that his name be entered on the muster roll, received two hundred dollars.

Shortly before Albert Gallatin caved in to Luke Wheeler's threats of legal action, a minor functionary in the navy office who was routinely updating the pay records came upon an almost forgotten name. Commodore James Barron had, as of February 8, 1813, completed the terms of his five-year suspension from the service, and as of that day was once again reinstated on the pay books, and was entitled to draw half pay of fifty dollars per month.

THIRTEEN

Gales Ferry

From the Royal Navy's perspective, the opening months of the war with America were little short of disaster. Time and again in single-ship actions the little American navy handed the British one defeat after another in an unbroken skein of victories that astonished the world and mortified the Admiralty: *Essex* versus *Alert, Constitution* versus *Guerriere, Wasp* versus *Frolic, United States* versus *Macedonian, Constitution* (again) versus *Java, Hornet* versus *Peacock.*

The editors of Britain's leading naval journal, *The Pilot,* read the statistics and despaired:

> *Can these statements be true; and can the English people hear them unmoved? Anyone who would have predicted such a result of an American war this time last year would have been treated as a madman or a traitor. He would have been told, if his opponents had condescended to argue with him, that long ere seven months had elapsed the American flag would be swept from the seas, the contemptible navy of the United States annihilated, and their maritime arsenals rendered a heap of ruins. Yet down to this moment not a single American frigate has struck her flag. They insult and laugh at our want of enterprise and vigour. They leave their ports when they please, and return to them when it suits their convenience; they traverse the Atlantic; they beset the West India Islands; they advance to the very chops of the Channel; they parade upon the coast of South America; nothing chases, nothing engages them but to yield them triumph.*

Of course, such a record of victories could not be sustained indefinitely. The American navy might be fierce, but it was also very small, and inevitably the world's largest and most powerful navy would strike back. The Lords of the Admiralty had hundreds of warships at their disposal. All they had to do was to detach a few from blockade duty off the coast of Napoleon's Europe and send them across the ocean to deal with the obstreperous Yankees.

Secretary of the Navy William Jones defined the situation clearly enough in a circular he sent out to his commodores on February 22, 1813:

"There is good reason to expect a very considerable augmentation of the naval force of the enemy on our coast the ensuing Spring," he warned, "& it will be perceived that his policy will be to blockade our Ships of War in our own harbors; intercepting our private cruisers, prizes and trade, and Harrass the seaboard." The solution was not to fight the Royal Navy, he told his readers, but to attack Britain's commerce.

> *Our great inferiority in naval strength does not permit us to meet them on this ground without hazarding the precious Germ of our national glory,—we have however the means of creating a powerful diversion, & of turning the Scale of annoyance against the enemy. It is therefore intended to dispatch all our public ships, now in Port, as soon as possible in such positions as may be best adapted to destroy the Commerce of the enemy, from the Cape of Goodhope, to Cape Clear, and continue out as long as the means of subsistence can be procured abroad, in any quarter. . . . Cruizing singly will also afford to our gallant Commanders a fair opportunity of displaying distinctly their Judgement, skill & enterprize, and of reaping the laurel of Fame, and its solid appendages.*

This last was a not particularly subtle reference to prize money.

From his cabin in the *United States,* lying at New York, Decatur wrote back on March 10, 1813, laying out an ambitious plan that would take him south to the Carolina coast and then north again and across the Atlantic.

"I shall be in the track of all the British Commerce returning from beyond the Cape of Good Hope from the Brazils & the West Indies and shall probably find their Merchantmen separated from their convoys as they commonly are dispersed before they have so far completed ther voyage home."

It would be a long cruise. "From the information I have of the preparation of the enemy there is no doubt that our whole coast will be lined with his men of war during the summer months—This presents but little difficulty to our going out but will render our return during the mild season extremely hazardous—I would prefer to remain out as long as possible & by all means untill the approach of the autumnal equinox when the attention of the Enemy will be occupied in providing for his own safety. To enable me to do this I will take between three and four months provisions."

Along with his *United States,* there were two other warships in New York waiting to get to sea. One was the sloop of war *Hornet,* which had so recently defeated HMS *Peacock,* and which was now under the command of James Biddle. The other was the navy's proudest new addition, the USS *Macedonian,* Decatur's trophy ship, newly refurbished and under the command of Captain Jacob Jones. All three captains had their own sailing orders, but they agreed to form a temporary squadron under Decatur, the better to punch their way through the blockade. Once at sea, they would go their separate ways, each to harass the enemy in a different corner of the ocean. Each man was confident of success, but the gods of battle, who had so recently smiled upon Decatur, were about to demonstrate their fickle nature.

Early in May 1813 the little squadron ventured out of New York's southern mouth and were lying off Sandy Hook awaiting a favorable wind when they spotted a seventy-four-gun British ship of the line on the horizon, accompanied by a frigate. The British ships made no attempt to move on the squadron, and seemed content to remain offshore, but near enough to keep an eye on the Americans.

Decatur held back. The blockaders carried too much firepower for the Americans to challenge them directly, but given a lucky shift in the weather there was still a chance they might manage to elude them in the dark and escape into the open sea. For several days the Americans remained at anchor off the Jersey coast hoping for a storm, but when it failed to materialize, Decatur reluctantly ordered his ships back into the harbor. They would try to get out of New York through the city's eastern exit, by way of Long Island Sound.

The three ships made their way through the turbulent crosscurrents of the Hell Gate and traversed the length of the sound. By the end of the month they were lying off Fishers Island, ready to make a dash through the Race, the narrow tidal channel that formed the mouth of Long Island Sound. Decatur consulted local fishermen, who warned him that there was greater British activity than normal in the area. He put his ships on heightened alert, and on the first day of June decided to make his move. Riding the swift-flowing tide, the three vessels sped through the Race and into the Atlantic. Far to the south they could see a British ship of the line and a frigate patrolling off the tip of Montauk Point. As soon as the Americans appeared, the enemy vessels immediately wore and gave chase. Decatur was not concerned and gave the signal to proceed. Given the great distance the British had to cover and his own ships' superior speed, he felt confident he could evade them. But moments later the little squadron found itself facing a more immediate threat when a lookout reported two more sail off the south end of Block Island, immediately in their path. Suddenly the waters were crawling with enemy ships. Decatur was forced to change plans again, and with no time to spare, he gave the order to regain the Race and make a dash for New London.

With little of the exuberance that had characterized American actions in the preceding months of victories, the three ships scrambled back ignominiously into Long Island Sound and made for the Thames River and New London. One of the blockaders managed to get close enough to exchange a few shots with the *United States,* but the Americans had a considerable head start and were able to reach safety before the British could cut them off.

And so began what was to prove the most frustrating year in Stephen Decatur's life. His three ships represented almost a fifth of the entire American fleet, and the British navy, delighted to have bottled up such a large and valuable segment of the American navy, immediately established a tight blockade of New London. Within a week Decatur could count two 74s and two thirty-eight-gun frigates lying off the coast. Any thoughts of a quick escape were clearly out of the question. While his decision to seek the shelter of New London harbor and the protection of its two forts may have saved his vessels from capture, it also effectively took them out of the war.

There was an immediate threat that the British, with their superior weight of metal, might choose to sail directly into the harbor and attack the American squadron where it lay. To protect his ships against such an eventuality he moved them up the river about five miles to a place called Gales Ferry and anchored them near an old trading post. There they lay in a wide and shallow bay tucked behind a bend in the river, sheltered by a high rocky ridge. It was virtually impossible for any of the British blockading vessels to get that far upriver, but to further protect his ships he stretched a heavy chain across the Thames to act as a barrier. On top of the hill, which had a commanding view of New London harbor and Long Island Sound beyond it, his crews built a fort and armed it with guns laboriously hauled up from the ships below. And there they waited for an attack that never came.

Decatur's effectiveness as a warrior had always been totally dependent on his ships—it was their speed, their firepower, and their ability to surprise and overwhelm that gave him power over his nation's enemies. Deprived of his freedom to bring his ships to battle, he was reduced to impotence.

Yet there was a doggedness in his character that simply refused to give in and admit the obvious. Time and again, throughout his year of imprisonment in his own country, he sought ways to fight back, to take charge, to impose his will upon events. His efforts were at times ingenious, at times farsighted, at times almost comic. Their only common characteristic was that they all failed.

One of his first acts after insuring his squadron's security was to seek the help of his friend and sometime business partner, the New York inventor Robert Fulton. Fulton is remembered today primarily for developing a practical steamboat, but his main interest for many years lay in the arcane technology of underwater warfare. He had experimented extensively with submarines in Europe and America and had developed a variety of underwater bomb devices, which he called "torpedoes." They were similar to what today would be called underwater mines and were powerful enough to blow a hole in any wooden ship and sink it, if the attacker could find some way to bring the torpedo into contact with the ship's hull. Fulton's torpedoes could be delivered to their targets by various means and detonated by a variety of fuses. Fulton himself suggested that the most efficient method of delivering a torpedo to an enemy vessel at anchor might be by means of a simple rowboat, operating at night with muffled oars.

When Fulton promised to supply sufficient torpedoes to threaten the blockading squadron, Decatur immediately set about recruiting volunteer torpedoists from among the local sea captains. They had been sitting at home in enforced idleness as a result of the blockade and were more than eager to try to blow up some of the British warships lying off New London, particularly since Congress promised them huge awards of prize money should their efforts succeed. With Fulton's help Decatur trained the volunteers and supplied them with the necessary watertight explosives. As a result of his efforts, there were a number of mysterious offshore explosions in and around the blockading squadron over the summer and autumn of 1813, as Connecticut patriots sought to sink the Royal Navy's capital ships with the help of Mr. Fulton's infernal machines. All failed.

One of Decatur's more fanciful attempts to influence events was his scheme to kidnap Captain Sir Thomas Masterman Hardy, the commander of the blockading squadron. Hardy had been Lord Nelson's flag captain at the Battle of Trafalgar, and his close association with England's greatest naval hero had made him famous throughout the British Empire. He was probably the best-known officer in the entire Royal Navy, and his capture, if it could be arranged, would cause a sensation. Decatur learned that Hardy regularly took his meals on land, at the home of John Lyon Gardiner, the American owner of Gardiner's Island, off the end of Long Island. Decatur developed a plan to surprise Hardy at dinner, spirit him away, and hold him for ransom. He would demand the freedom of his squadron as the price for the return of the famous captain.

In retrospect, the scheme reads like adolescent hijinks, but it was in fact a well-thought-out plan, and only failed when the little band of kidnappers, who had secreted themselves overnight on Gardiner's Island, ended up catching Hardy's squad of bodyguards before they could get to Hardy himself. Lumbered with a squad of British seamen who had no ransom value whatsoever, the kidnappers were forced to flee before they could even get to Hardy, and the project failed. Needless to say, Captain Hardy made sure Decatur never got a second chance. He returned to the practice of taking his meals on board his flagship, HMS *Ramillies,* where he was surrounded by five hundred British tars and protected by a sufficient battery of guns to discourage any further attempts on his freedom.

One of the few bright spots during that long and frustrating summer of 1813 was Oliver Hazard Perry's September 10 victory on Lake Erie, heralded by his triumphant message that quickly became celebrated throughout the nation: "We have met the enemy and they are ours, two ships, two brigs, one schooner and one sloop." Cheered by news of the victory, Decatur ordered a salute of eighteen guns fired—one gun for each state in the union—and an extra tot of grog for the men.

By October, Decatur was ready to try to make a break for it, regardless of the greater strength of Hardy's squadron. "The enemy off here keep a vigilant lookout for us," he wrote the secretary of the navy, "but I indulge a hope that we shall soon be able to avoid them and get to sea." In preparation for the attempt, he brought his three ships back down to the harbor, where they would be ready to escape at a moment's notice should the opportunity present itself. Decatur knew the British maintained an active spy network in New London—Captain Hardy always seemed to be aware of his most secret plans—and he knew that the news of his return to New London would soon reach the blockaders, but he did not plan to make his escape immediately and hoped the continued presence of the American ships in the harbor over a period of weeks would eventually make them such a familiar sight that they would no longer cause notice.

He selected the night of December 12 for his escape. There would be no moon and the tides were favorable. Late that night he was about to weigh anchor in utmost secrecy when a lookout reported blue signal lights burning on either side of the river mouth, obviously put there to warn the enemy of his planned escape. Furious but resigned to his fate, Decatur abandoned the attempt. "Notwithstanding, these signals have been repeated," he wrote angrily to the secretary a few days later, "and have been seen by twenty persons at least in the squadron, there are men in New London who have the hardihood to affect to disbelieve it, and the effrontery to avow their disbelief."

One of Decatur's most curious escape plans surfaced in January 1814, when he tried to interest the British blockaders in participating in a pair of ship duels between the two American frigates, the *United States* and the

Macedonian, and their British counterparts in the blockading squadron, the *Endymion,* a new arrival similar in size and armament to the American super frigates, and the *Statira,* a sister of the *Macedonian.*

At first, Captain Hardy seemed agreeable to such a pair of life-or-death contests, to be fought somewhere off Montauk Point, but he soon had second thoughts. The scheme—which in retrospect was little short of loopy—quickly fell apart.

By early spring 1814 the secretary of the navy had had enough. He was desperate to have his most effective commander back at sea, and lost all hope that Decatur could find a way out of New London. He ordered him to take his ships back upriver once again and dismantle them. Their war was over.

He offered Decatur command of either the *Guerriere,* a brand new frigate soon to be launched at Philadelphia, or the *President,* the third of America's super frigates, which was then lying at New York. Decatur chose the latter, because of its reputation for speed. "The well known rapidity of the *President'*s sailing places her in my estimation above all the others," he wrote back. "I think her opportunity for proceeding to sea much better than the *Guerriere'*s. . . . Having been so long blockaded, I dread being placed in such an unpleasant situation."

With his little squadron safely tucked away up the Thames, Decatur prepared to lead his crew overland to New York and take command of the *President.* But there was one last task remaining before he could leave his Connecticut prison. The secretary of the navy ordered him to preside over a court-martial of the surviving officers of that most unfortunate of ships, the *Chesapeake.* The record of the court-martial tells us more about Decatur's state of mind after his year of inactivity than the entire list of his failed escape efforts.

A year earlier, on the very day that Decatur had been forced to take shelter in New London, the USS *Chesapeake* had set out from Boston on what would prove her last cruise as an American frigate. She was under the command of the dashing Captain James Lawrence, who was determined to attack HMS *Shannon,* a thirty-eight-gun frigate on blockade duty off the city. The entire exercise was an act of folly on Lawrence's part. He and his ship were totally unprepared. He had been in command of the *Chesapeake* for less than two weeks and barely knew the officers and men, most of whom were as new to the ship as himself. Some had come aboard only the day before departure. There had been no time to train the crew. But Lawrence was unconcerned. He was totally disdainful of the British and convinced of his own invulnerability.

The two ships met about eighteen miles off Boston light. They were evenly matched in terms of size, firepower, and speed, but in a brief and fiercely fought action that lasted less than fifteen minutes, the *Shannon,* thanks to masterful seamanship and superb gunnery, simply overwhelmed the *Chesapeake*. Lawrence was mortally struck in the opening moments, and a full third of his crew was either killed or wounded. The battle was over almost before it began, the first American naval defeat of the war.

Now, almost a year later, Decatur would preside over a court-martial of the *Chesapeake*'s surviving officers, who had been returned to the United States in an exchange of prisoners. The first officer tried was Acting Lieutenant William Cox, a nineteen-year-old midshipman and the senior unwounded survivor. Cox had joined the *Chesapeake* only two days before the battle and had been assigned to command a division of eighteen-pounders on her gun deck. His orders were to fight his battery until he heard the bugle call for boarders, at which point he was to lead his men to the quarterdeck and join an assault party that would attempt to carry the enemy's ship.

When the action began between the *Shannon* and the *Chesapeake* Cox found his guns were on the disengaged side of the ship, so he had nothing to do. He ordered his men to follow him to the quarterdeck in anticipation of the call for boarders. He was the first man out of the hatch, and even at that early stage of the battle, he found the deck in a state of chaos, with all the principal officers, including Captain Lawrence, dead or wounded. The *Chesapeake*'s sailors were milling around in dazed confusion. No one was at the wheel. Although he did not realize it, Cox was at that point the commanding officer of the *Chesapeake*.

Captain Lawrence, still conscious, begged to be taken below to his cabin. Cox rounded up a couple of sailors and the three moved him below as best they could. As they passed down the hatch, Lawrence exhorted the crew, "Don't give up the ship!" In the cabin, while Cox tried to make his captain as comfortable as possible, a sailor came in with a message from his wounded superior, Lieutenant Budd, ordering him to take command of the ship. Cox hurried out fully intending to comply with the order, but when he tried to get back to the quarterdeck he was blocked by crowds of panicked sailors trying to escape from the British boarders. By the time he finally got past them, the colors had been struck and the British were in control of the ship.

The loss of the *Chesapeake* was in large measure a pointless and unnecessary tragedy brought on by the bravado of a vain and overconfident James Lawrence, who had acted recklessly in bringing on the action. But Lawrence, even in defeat, was a public hero, and his "Don't give up the ship!" became a popular battle cry. The dead Lawrence might be the guilty party, but someone else would have to shoulder the blame. The court decided it was to be Lieutenant Cox. He was convicted of neglect of duty and unofficerlike conduct and sentenced "to be cashiered with a perpetual incapacity to serve in the Navy of the United States."

It was an obviously unfair decision, given Cox's youth and lack of training, but Stephen Decatur was not particularly interested in fairness or even justice. He was interested only in developing and maintaining a corps of zealous, quick-witted and determined naval officers. By his lights, Cox should have intuitively understood that in the heat of battle there is no time to comfort the wounded, even if the wounded person is your captain and a national hero.

There was little room for compassion in Decatur's navy, either for others or, as it would turn out, for himself.

FOURTEEN

USS President *and* *HMS* Endymion

O n his arrival in New York, Decatur was impatient to get the *President* to sea as soon as possible. After almost a year as a virtual prisoner of the British navy, he was eager to get back in the fight. But this time it was the British army that foiled his plans. Following the surrender of Napoleon, thousands of British troops in Europe had been hurriedly transported across the Atlantic to take part in the American war, and in the summer of 1814 the enemy opened a new and worrying series of land attacks on the entire eastern coast of the country. British army forces, supported by the Royal Navy, invaded and occupied large sections of northern Maine, forcing the inhabitants to swear allegiance to the king, and when other British troops burned Washington and bombarded Baltimore, Decatur was ordered to organize the defenses of New York and Philadelphia, in the expectation of enemy attacks against those ports as well.

It was not until the end of the year, when the bitter North American winter made army campaigning impractical, that he was finally free to get away. His sailing orders called for an extended cruise halfway around the world to the Bay of Bengal, where he planned to attack the rich commercial trade of the British East India Company.

First, of course, he would have to get past the blockade. The British squadron off New York consisted of four principal vessels, the *Majestic,* a ship of the line that had been razeed (shaved down) to a single-deck warship of fifty-six guns, the *Endymion,* forty guns, and two thirty-eight-gun frigates, the *Pomone* and the *Tenedos.* Under the command of Captain John Hayes, the squadron maintained a tight control over the harbor that made escape under normal conditions virtually impossible. Decatur recognized he would have to wait for a spell of foul weather to help him out.

Finally, on January 14, 1815, the storm he was looking for arrived out of the west. Strong gales propelled an early blizzard into the city and forced the blockaders off their station and out to sea. As the howling winds increased, Decatur decided to make his move under cover of darkness. Late in the afternoon he left his anchorage off Staten Island and dropped down to Sandy Hook, where he would wait to cross the bar with the rising tide, about eight o'clock that evening.

What neither Decatur nor the men in charge of the blockading squadron could know was that the war they were fighting was already over, and had been over for three weeks. British and American negotiators meeting in Belgium had signed a peace treaty on Christmas Eve, which had then been ratified by the Prince Regent in London on December 28. The treaty had been immediately dispatched to the United States on board HMS *Favourite,* which was still on the high seas, battling the same storm that had blown the blockaders off station, and which Decatur was preparing to enter.

As night fell the weather cleared but the gale-force winds continued undiminished, roiling the unprotected shallows where they were anchored. Because Decatur's sailing orders called for an unusually long cruise to the Indian Ocean, the frigate lay deep in the water, her hold packed with provisions. Decatur had hired local pilots to get the *President* over the bar, guided by marker boats illuminated with shielded lights that had been set out earlier in the day to indicate the channel. A little after eight o'clock, with the tide rising, the *President* weighed anchor and with storm sails set moved cautiously forward. Almost immediately disaster struck. Either through pilot error or because of a misplaced marker boat, the ship, with a great shuddering lurch that could be felt from stem to stern, missed the channel and struck the bar hard. She was suddenly helplessly aground, immobilized and at the mercy of the storm. Decatur and his crew tried frantically to free her, jettisoning nonessentials and rocking the ship by organizing the entire crew to run from side to side in unison, but all to no avail. For an hour and a half the *President* was pounded by winds and high seas that twisted her keel, broke several of her rudder braces, and split her masts. The constant battering forced open the planking and started leaks. The storm was permanently damaging the ship, and Decatur's first thought was to somehow try to back her off the bar and return to port, but the strong offshore gale made that impossible.

At around ten o'clock that night the flood tide surged and finally lifted the *President* over the bar and out to sea. Although the ship was severely crippled, there was no going back. Decatur had no choice but to proceed eastward into the dark. His people spent the rest of the night inspecting the ship, assessing the damage as best they could in the darkness, and making whatever temporary repairs were possible. She had developed major leaks and there was noticeable hull distortion. The keel had been severely hogged, or twisted, which affected her sailing and slowed her down.

But the worst news still lay ahead. At first light, around five o'clock in the morning, with the ship now some fifty miles east of Sandy Hook, lookouts spotted two sails directly ahead. Almost certainly they were part of the blockading squadron. Decatur managed to pass them to windward undetected, but an hour later they spotted him and turned in chase. When other sails appeared over the horizon, there could no longer be any question of their identity. Soon Decatur found himself trying to outrun the entire blockading squadron that he had tried so desperately to evade. The *Majestic, Endymion, Tenedos,* and *Pomone* were not more than two miles distant.

For hour after hour in the bitter cold, with icicles encasing the shrouds and rigging, Decatur managed to hold his lead, but due to the damage the ship had sustained on the bar, he was unable to increase his distance from his pursuers. The largest of the British ships, the *Majestic,* fired occasionally at the Americans, but without effect, and by midday she and the *Pomone* were falling behind, leaving *Endymion* to maintain the chase. The British ship was clearly faster than the *President,* but she deliberately remained behind her quarry, keeping out of range of Decatur's twenty-four-pounders. Now and then she yawed to bring her battery to bear, firing an occasional broadside at the *President* before returning to her previous position. Decatur, with his reduced speed, could not afford to answer back, except with his two stern chasers, which proved ineffective.

In a desperate attempt to increase speed, Decatur again gave the order to lighten ship, "starting the water, cutting away the anchors, throwing overboard provisions, cables, spare spars, boats, and every article that could be gotten at." Lightening a ship during a chase was always a highly delicate operation, since the emptying of half a dozen more water casks at one end of the ship than at the other could materially shift her trim and affect her seaworthiness. Decatur and his crew had never before been to sea in the *President* and were therefore unfamiliar with her sailing characteristics. Decatur knew he was taking a significant risk but with inevitable capture the only alternative, he had no option.

By three o'clock in the afternoon the other British vessels had fallen behind, and the *President* now had only the *Endymion* to contend with. The Americans were getting almost no wind, and were kept busy wetting their sails from the royals down, while the British, helped by a strong breeze, were able to position their ship at will. By five o'clock, a full twenty-four hours after the *President* had first set out from Staten Island, the *Endymion* came up within a quarter mile of Decatur. Both vessels were steering east by north with the wind on the larboard quarter, and the *Endymion* was now so positioned that she could maintain a concentrated fire from her larboard bow and bridle ports, while neither Decatur's stern chasers nor his quarter guns could be brought to bear.

Night was coming on. While Decatur knew that the other British ships could be expected to catch up eventually, his only immediate worry was the *Endymion*. In one of those highly imaginative, totally unorthodox insights that were so characteristic of him, he suddenly came up with an extraordinary plan of battle: he would escape the *Endymion* by capturing her—he would board her, carry her, and sail away in her, and scuttle the *President,* to boot!

He immediately ordered a howitzer hauled over to the main hatch and pointed down into it, ready to blow out the ship's bottom when the time came. Then he gathered his crew around him and explained his plan. "My lads, that ship is coming up with us. As our ship won't sail, we'll go on board of theirs, every man and boy of us, and carry her into New York. All I ask of you is to follow me!" Decatur's audacity was infectious, and the crew cheered in support.

The plan was unconventional, but not without precedent. In the Revolution, when John Paul Jones's *Bonnehomme Richard* began to sink during his victorious battle off Flamborough Head in the English Channel, he had abandoned ship, transferred his entire crew to his prize, HMS *Serapis,* and sailed away to France.

Boarding the *Endymion* was going to require some doing. The English frigate would have to close near enough to let the *President* sheer suddenly and board her before his intentions could be perceived. But whenever Decatur tried to haul nearer, the *Endymion* hauled off, and being the faster ship, always managed to evade him. As night fell Decatur regretfully abandoned his audacious scheme. But it was clear he would have to come up with something, and around six o'clock he abruptly changed course to the south, hoping to get his own broadside to bear, so that he might cripple the *Endymion* before the rest of her squadron came up. The *Endymion* bore away in response to Decatur's change of direction, and now the two warships were racing along on parallel courses in the dark, separated by less than a quarter mile and exchanging broadside for broadside, their visibility limited to the occasional flash of the guns.

They were almost precisely an even match, the *President* rated for forty-four guns and carrying fifty-two, and the *Endymion,* nominally a forty-gun ship and carrying fifty. On both ships, the main deck guns were twenty-four-pounders, with a shattering effect nearly twice that of the eighteen-pounders carried by standard frigates.

With the full broadsides brought into action, the casualties began to mount. One of the first was the *President*'s first lieutenant, Fitz Henry Babbitt. He was standing near the wheel when a thirty-two-pound carronade shot severed his right leg below the knee. The impact caused him to fall down the hatch to the gun deck, fracturing his right thigh in two places. This second injury made it impossible to move him or fix a tourniquet to his leg, and he lost so much blood he soon realized he could not survive. The pain must have been excruciating, but he spent the last two hours of his life dictating affectionate letters to his friends. He removed a miniature of his fiancée from around his neck with the request that it be returned, and before expiring, gave instruction that his pocket watch be sent as a parting memorial to his brother. The nobility of his death was typical of the manner in which naval officers of almost every nation chose to die in that era when a good death was as important as life itself.

The *Endymion*'s fire was rapid and accurate. Decatur was wounded in the chest by a large splinter that knocked him to the deck with such force that he momentarily lost consciousness. When he recovered, he picked himself up, only to be hit in the face by another, smaller splinter. Near seven o'clock he learned of the death of his fourth lieutenant, Archibald Hamilton, the young man who had carried the *Macedonian*'s ensign to Washington and laid it at the feet of Dolley Madison.

It was difficult for the men to see what they were doing. The only light on board the ship came from a few hooded lanterns. The men were forced to fight the guns in the gloom, adding an additional level of danger to their work. Both vessels carried an additional lantern at the mizzen peak to serve in lieu of their flags, which were still flying, but invisible in the dark.

By eight o'clock, the Americans noted that the fire from the *Endymion* had slackened measurably. A half hour later, with most of her larboard guns knocked off their carriages or otherwise disabled, the British ship ceased firing completely and began to drift helplessly. Her sails had been literally cut from her yards by the American guns, and with only a few tattered remnants left to catch the wind, she began to drop back and out of action.

The battle was over. The *Endymion* had stopped fighting, but she had not struck her colors. Her lantern still hung defiantly from her mizzen. For Decatur, it was a victory, a hard-won victory, but hardly a triumph.

Had he been engaged in a single-ship action, Decatur could have easily forced the *Endymion*'s surrender with a couple of additional broadsides—his own guns were in good order, and stood ready to continue the fight—but the two ships were not alone. There was the rest of the British squadron to consider, and they would soon catch up. Decatur did not want to be there when they arrived. He decided to make a dash for it, and told the man at the helm to return to the former course of east by north. He was so unintimidated by the *Endymion* that in turning he presented his stern—the most vulnerable part of his ship—to the Britisher's broadside. The *Endymion*'s guns remained silent.

The *President* headed off on her new course, leaving the *Endymion* dead in the water. As luck would have it, the Americans were quickly swallowed up by some dirty weather that effectively cloaked their movements from the other warships in the area. For two hours they plowed northward, and had started to hope they had made good their escape when the weather cleared once more and the bright stars overhead revealed the *Pomone* ranging up on the *President*'s larboard side, the *Tenedos* taking up a raking position on her starboard quarter, and the *Majestic,* accompanied by the brig *Dispatch,* closing up under her stern. Once again the British had found them.

It was now about eleven o'clock at night. Decatur and his crew had been awake since the morning of the day before, first fighting a pounding sea that threatened to destroy their ship on the bar, and then waging a running battle against an entire enemy squadron. "The *Pomone* had opened her fire on the starboard bow within musket shot," Decatur would write in his official report, "the other [HMS *Tenedos*] about two cables' length astern, taking a raking position on our quarter; and the rest, with the exception of the *Endymion,* within gunshot. Thus situated, with about one fifth of my crew killed or wounded, my ship crippled, and a more than fourfold force opposed to me, without a chance of escape left, I deemed it my duty to surrender."

For Decatur it must have been a moment of profound anguish, a bitter and unwelcome experience unprecedented in his remarkable career. He gave the order to haul down the lantern hanging at the mizzen peak, and the guns, both British and American, fell silent. While officers from the *Pomone* and *Tenedos* came on board to take possession of the *President,* remove prisoners, and assign a prize crew. Decatur took the opportunity to go below to the cockpit to visit the wounded and let the surgeon minister to his own injuries, which turned out to be broken ribs, painful but not particularly dangerous.

There was one last unwelcome duty to perform. He returned to his cabin and exchanged his farmer's clothes for his full uniform. He strapped on his sword, which he must soon surrender. The boat was waiting to carry him over to the *Majestic.* As he climbed painfully down into the stern-sheets, he could see that the *Endymion,* having bent a new set of sails, shifted her spars, and rove new running rigging, had come up and joined the others.

Captain John Hayes of the *Majestic,* as commander of the victorious squadron, refused to accept Decatur's sword and restored it to him with much the same formula that he himself had used in returning Carden's after the battle with the *Macedonian,* with words to the effect that "he felt proud in returning the sword of an officer who had defended his ship so gallantly."

In Bermuda, where he and his men were taken after the surrender, Decatur was treated as an honored guest at British headquarters, and Admiral Sir Alexander Cochrane, chief of the North American Station, gave a dinner in his honor. It was quickly arranged to send him home at the earliest possible date in HMS *Narcissus.* On his arrival at New London, which coincided with the news of the peace treaty, he was greeted as a hero and drawn through the streets in a carriage by cheering citizens.

When word of the loss of the *President* reached the Brooklyn Navy Yard, the ship carpenters volunteered to donate sixteen hundred days of work toward building a new frigate for him.

He was still the public's darling.

At the time, no one ever publicly questioned Decatur's decision to surrender the *President*. Both friend and foe alike hailed his gallantry and that of his crew and characterized his surrender to a superior force as inevitable and unavoidable. But what is abundantly clear is that Stephen Decatur did not share the prevailing opinion of his own actions. Almost from the moment of the surrender, he became obsessed with his own guilt and driven by the need to absolve himself. What others saw as honorable, he saw as shameful. He could not forget that he was the man who had boasted that "the flag of my country will never be struck while there is a hull for it to wave from." No matter the circumstances, no matter the number of enemy warships that bore upon him, the reality of his surrender made a mockery of his high rhetoric. Almost as soon as he returned to America, he petitioned the secretary of the navy to convene a court of inquiry of the "most distinguished men of the profession" in order to investigate his conduct in the loss of the *President*.

Such a board was duly empaneled, and after a careful consideration of the facts, was unequivocal in its support of Decatur. "We fear that we cannot express, in a manner that will do justice to our feelings, our admiration of the conduct of Commodore Decatur, and his officers and crew, while engaged with the enemy, threatened with a force so superior, possessing advantages which must have appeared to render all opposition unavailing, other wise than might affect the honor of our navy, and the character of our seamen. They fought with a spirit, which no prospect of success could have heightened, and if victory had met its common reward, the *Endymion*'s name would have been added to our list of naval conquests. In this unequal conflict, the enemy gained a ship, but the victory was ours."

———

It was not until 1882, almost seventy years after the battle, that Theodore Roosevelt, then a young Harvard graduate researching the naval War of 1812, studied all the documents relating to the action, both British and American, and published his assessment, which suggested that while Decatur had clearly vanquished the *Endymion,* he had just as clearly surrendered too soon. "It is difficult to see how any outsider with an ounce of common-sense and fairmindedness can help awarding the palm to Decatur, as regards the action with the *Endymion.* But I regret to say that . . . he acted rather tamely, certainly not heroically, in striking to the *Pomone.* There was, of course, not much chance of success in doing battle with two fresh frigates; but then they only mounted eighteen-pounders, and . . . it would have been rather a long time before they would have caused much damage. Meanwhile . . . A lucky shot might have disabled one of her opponents, and then the other would, in all probability, have undergone the same fate as the *Endymion.* At least it was well worth trying."

There were those who faulted the bumptious young Roosevelt, ridiculing him for sitting by a cozy fire, reading the old records, and deciding whether a half-frozen, wounded, and sleep-deprived commander standing in the dark on a deck covered in ice and blood should have continued fighting or not, but the fact was Roosevelt had a point. Decatur could never have vanquished the entire blockading squadron, and his surrender was inevitable, but it is not beyond imagination to think that the *President,* with her battery of twenty-four-pounders, could have finished off one of the eighteen-pounder frigates before lowering her colors to an undeniably superior force.

Decatur's sense of guilt over the surrender of the *President* would serve as the motivation for what he always considered the crowning achievement of his career, when he returned later that year to the Barbary shore and the scenes of his first glory.

FIFTEEN

"Dove Mi Piace!"

While still a prisoner in Bermuda, Decatur had written a letter to Commodore Richard Dale in which he made clear how heavily the surrender of the *President* weighed upon him. At first he wrote "I have lost a noble ship, sir, but I hope it will be considered there has been no loss of honor." Then, in a particularly revealing afterthought, he struck out the phrase "it will be considered," and in its place wrote "I shall satisfy the world." Just how he planned to satisfy the world remained unclear, but events were moving quickly, and circumstances would soon provide the opportunity to make good his proud boast.

President Madison and his new secretary of the navy, Benjamin Crowninshield, were both well aware of Decatur's continued anxiety over his possible loss of public favor, and each was immensely distressed by it. They were going to need his unique talents for the country's next foreign enterprise, which would involve a return to the Mediterranean. The Barbary state of Algiers had taken advantage of America's preoccupation with its war with Britain to break its treaty with the United States and return to its old plundering ways of capturing Yankee merchantmen and throwing their crews into slavery. Madison was furious, and as soon as the peace treaty with Britain was ratified he persuaded Congress to declare war on Algiers. America now had a powerful new navy, and Madison wanted to send it to Algiers and force the dey to respect the American flag, and he wanted Decatur to play a leading part in the operation.

Even before the court of inquiry got around to exonerating Decatur for the loss of the *President*, Crowninshield sent a highly unusual private letter to him, disclosing plans for sending two separate squadrons to the Mediterranean. One was to set out as soon as possible, while the other would join it later that summer. Crowninshield offered him the command of either the frigate *Guerriere* in the first squadron, or the brand new seventy-four-gun ship of the line *George Washington* in the second. If neither assignment appealed to him, the secretary offered him the post of commandant of the Charlestown Navy Yard in Boston harbor. Crowninshield closed his letter warmly: "In short, my dear sir, your wishes are to be consulted. Any service or any station that is at the disposal of this Department rely upon it, you may command."

Decatur was recuperating from his broken ribs at Bradish's boarding house in New York, and he discussed Crowninshield's offer with his fellow lodger and friend, the popular author and wit Washington Irving. Both men agreed that the navy yard post was out of the question. Decatur could only recoup his laurels where he had first won them, in the Mediterranean. But with which squadron should he sail?

Crowninshield's letter explained that the second squadron was to be led by Commodore William Bainbridge. Decatur had no quarrel with that. Bainbridge was a friend and deserved the opportunity to pay back the Barbary pirates for the hardships and humiliations they had inflicted on him. But there was no question that Bainbridge's involvement in the enterprise presented a problem for Decatur. Bainbridge was Decatur's senior in rank by almost four years, and would automatically assume overall command when the two squadrons met, and Decatur was in no mood to accept a secondary position.

Washington Irving urged him to take command of the first squadron, to make a "brilliant dash" of it, and to "whip the cream off the enterprise" before Bainbridge, who was in Boston fitting out America's first ship of the line, the seventy-four-gun USS *Independence,* arrived in the Mediterranean. Decatur agreed. It might mean stealing Bainbridge's thunder, but friendship would have to take second place to the pursuit of glory. It was the opportunity to redeem himself that he was looking for, and he immediately wrote Crowninshield accepting the position of commander-in-chief of the first squadron, with the new frigate *Guerriere* as his flagship. He requested that those of his old officers and crew who wished to follow him into his new ship be allowed to do so, and included one significant proviso—that he be permitted to leave the Mediterranean the moment the two squadrons merged. "Notwithstanding my desire for active employment is great I should prefer remaining on shore to taking a situation as second in the fleet now going to the Mediterranean. I have commanded a Squadron for nearly 8 years. To take a subordinate station in my present situation might be considered as an evidence of the Government's confidence having been withdrawn from me." As always, Decatur made no bones about his sensitivity to appearances. He never lost sight of the fact that his power lay in public approval.

Crowninshield endorsed all of Decatur's conditions, and by return mail encouraged him to depart "without delay." Decatur did not disappoint him.

Working around the clock, Decatur managed to fit out and provision a squadron of ten sail in New York in a startlingly brief span of time, and on May 20 set sail for the Mediterranean. His squadron was the largest fleet of American warships ever assembled up to that time, and presented a magnificent sight parading out through the Narrows—his flagship, the super frigate *Guerriere,* his personal trophy ship, the *Macedonian,* and the frigate *Constellation,* the sloop *Ontario,* the brigs *Epervier, Firefly, Flambeau,* and *Spark,* and the schooners *Spitfire* and *Torch.*

With him on board the *Guerriere* was William Shaler, a veteran merchant captain and diplomat who had been assigned by the State Department to write the treaties with the North African dependencies.

Decatur's plan of action was simple. If at all possible, he hoped to capture an Algerine corsair before entering into negotiations with the dey. Such a victory would undoubtedly help convince the Algerines that America was resolved to stop their predations. Once the squadron was east of the Azores, Decatur ordered extra lookouts to search for any strange sail.

When he touched at Cadiz, he learned from the American consul that an Algerine squadron had in fact been in the Atlantic, but was now thought to be active in the Mediterranean. The intelligence was later confirmed by the consul at Tangier, who informed Decatur that the celebrated Algerine admiral Reis Hammida had touched there just two days earlier in his flagship, the frigate *Mashouda,* and had since then passed up the Mediterranean. On June 15, when Decatur reached Gibraltar, he learned that he could probably find Hammida off Cape de Gatte, where he would be waiting for a tribute payment of half a million dollars from the Spanish government. Decatur immediately ordered his ships eastward.

It was at Gibraltar that Decatur's legend collected yet another anecdote. A group of British naval officers was watching the ships make their way around the bay when one asked an American who was present for the names of the different vessels. The American pointed to the commodore's flagship and said, "That sir, is the *Guerriere,*" and then, pointing to another frigate, "and that is the *Macedonian,*" and then pointing to one of the sloops, identified her as the *Epervier.* "The next, sir, is—" "Oh, damn the next!" grumbled the angry English officer, chagrined on hearing the names of three Royal Navy ships that had been captured by the Americans.

Two days after departing Gibraltar, while sailing about twenty miles off the Spanish coast, Decatur found what he was looking for. A large sail was spotted toward the southeast, and as the Americans grew near, she proved to be the same Algerine frigate described by the consul at Tangier. Decatur ordered the Americans to display English colors to hide their true identity, but the stranger, sensing danger, was not so easily fooled and made every effort to get away. A cloud of canvas blossomed over her tops as if by magic, and she began making rapid headway on a southerly course, bound toward Algiers, hundreds of miles over the horizon. It was a display of superb seamanship not lost on Decatur's men. "Quicker work was never done by better seamen," an impressed American officer reported.

But there was to be no escape. Decatur had an entire squadron at his command, and the Americans simply mobbed the frigate. It was the same situation Decatur had faced in the *President,* only in reverse, and after twenty-five minutes of concentrated action, the *Mashouda* signaled her surrender. When the Americans went on board, they found the usual carnage and learned that the fierce and justly feared Admiral Hammida had been killed in one of the first broadsides, cut in two by a forty-two-pound carronade shot.

The capture presented Decatur with over four hundred prisoners, and he ordered his prize crew to sail the *Mashouda* to Cartagena and land them there, where it would be easier to hold them. He did not expect to keep them long.

Two days later the Americans came on an Algerine brig sailing close inshore, and captured her when she ran aground trying to escape. She was the *Estedio,* of twenty-two guns, and while many of her sailors managed to scramble ashore and get away, Decatur's men managed to capture about eighty of them. As soon as the Americans refloated the brig, Decatur threw a second prize crew on board and ordered her into Cartagena as well. With two captured warships and almost five hundred prisoners he now had a wealth of bargaining chips with which to negotiate. Without further ado, he turned toward Algiers. It had been only thirty days since he left New York.

On June 28, with every ship prominently displaying American colors, the squadron arrived off Algiers. The following morning Decatur ordered a white flag of truce hoisted to the *Guerriere's* foremast head, and a Swedish flag at the main, thus signaling to the dey's people that he had come to negotiate and that he wished to carry out the negotiations through the Swedish consul in Algiers, a Mr. Norderling. Around noon a boat put out from town carrying Mr. Norderling and the Algerine captain of the port. On reaching the *Guerriere,* the two emissaries were welcomed on board by Decatur and Mr. Shaler.

The captain of the port recognized Decatur by name. His reputation was still very much alive along the Barbary coast. At the bargaining table

Decatur opened negotiations by informing his guests of the capture of the *Mashouda* and *Estedio* and the death of Admiral Hammida. When the captain of the port refused to believe him, Decatur sent for one of Hammida's lieutenants, who confirmed the news to the shocked official. The two Americans then presented a letter from President Madison to the dey offering the choice of war, or peace on American terms. When the port captain suggested that discussions might be more appropriately carried out on land, at accommodations closer to the dey's palace, Decatur refused, and insisted that all negotiations were to take place on board the *Guerriere*. He was going to run the show, and there were to be no questions on that score.

The next morning the captain of the port and the Swedish consul returned to the *Guerriere,* this time with authorization from the dey to negotiate in his name. The Americans presented them with a draft treaty put together by Shaler and Decatur that called for an inviolable and universal peace and friendship between the president of the United States and the dey of Algiers and their respective citizens and subjects. There was a clause calling for most favored nation status, and another calling for the permanent cessation of any form of annual tribute. The Americans knew this provision was likely to make the dey particularly unhappy, since it struck at the very heart of the Barbary economy, which was based on extortion. They hoped to sweeten the bitter pill with another clause that called for the immediate exchange of all prisoners held by the two parties. Since the dey was holding about ten American prisoners against the five hundred Decatur was holding, it was hoped that the clause might ameliorate the pain imposed by the ban on tribute.

The captain of the port suggested that a token annual tribute of naval stores, including a little gunpowder, might make the treaty more acceptable to the dey, but Decatur would have none of it. "If you insist on receiving powder as tribute," Decatur remarked dryly, "you must expect to receive cannonballs with it."

The parties came to a crucial point in the negotiations when the Algerine demanded that the two warships captured by Decatur be returned.

Shaler politely refused to make such a promise. He was an experienced diplomat and understood the problems inherent in such a pledge. Both of the captured warships were at that time in Cartagena, a Spanish port, and therefore under Spanish control. The United States government's claim to the *Mashouda* as a legitimate prize of war was clear, but the *Estedio* had been captured within Spanish territorial waters and Shaler could not presume American title to the brig. For that reason, he explained, his government could not make the promise the dey's representative demanded.

The Algerine warned the Americans that he could not assure the dey's agreement to the treaty unless the two ships were returned. Shaler again refused to pledge the return of the ships, and was supported by the Swedish consul. Decatur grew restless. The negotiations threatened to degenerate into a discussion of diplomatic technicalities that could easily stretch out into weeks of nitpicking and counterclaims. He could not allow the talks to founder. He wanted an agreement, and he wanted it right away if he was to "whip the cream off the enterprise," as Washington Irving had urged him to do. He interrupted the negotiations to make an extraordinary offer. If Shaler could not promise the return of the ships, then he, Commodore Stephen Decatur, would personally guarantee their return.

Both Shaler and the Swedish consul were shocked. They understood the complexity of the issue that Decatur seemed so willing to ignore. They tried to dissuade him, but Decatur was adamant, and his name and reputation carried such weight that when the final treaty was presented to the dey, along with Decatur's separate guarantee for the return of the ships, he agreed to the terms without further changes. By the end of the day the treaty was signed, and William Shaler had been invited by the dey to move ashore immediately and take up his duties as consul general for the Barbary states.

The date was June 30, six weeks after his squadron left New York, and Decatur had personally negotiated a landmark treaty that gave the United States more favorable terms than the Algerine government had ever granted to any state outside the Ottoman Empire. The dey had agreed to

such humiliating conditions for one reason, Decatur wrote proudly to Secretary Crowninshield, and that was that the treaty "had been dictated at
the mouth of the cannon." He added that "the presence of a respectable
naval force in this sea will be the certain guarantee for its observance."

Having forced the dey to come to terms, Decatur was eager to teach a
similar lesson to those other troublesome Barbary leaders, the bey of
Tunis and the bashaw of Tripoli. But some members of his crew were
beginning to show signs of scurvy, so before proceeding up the North
African coast the squadron stopped for ten days at Caligari, on the southern extremity of Sardinia, for rest and refreshment.

When Decatur eventually brought his squadron before Tunis on July
26 he found the bey and his advisors were as stubborn in their refusal to
negotiate as the Algerines had been. But Decatur was in command of an
overwhelming force and was no longer constrained by William Shaler's
diplomatic niceties. He quickly forced the bey to accede to his demands,
and with this second agreement signed and in hand, he moved on to
Tripoli. Within a week, using similar strong-arm methods, he obtained
from the bashaw still a third signed agreement.

By August 7, just seventy-nine days after his departure from New
York, he had accomplished everything that his government had sought,
and except for the sea battles with the *Mashouda* and *Estedio,* he had done it
all without firing a shot in anger. The mere threat of force had been sufficient. The cruise had been, by any measure, a spectacular success.

On July 31, exactly one month after Decatur's whirlwind diplomacy had
secured peace with Algiers, Commodore William Bainbridge, his pennant
proudly hoisted in America's first line of battleship, the USS *Independence,*
arrived at Gibraltar at the head of the second Mediterranean squadron,
eager to confront the wily Algerines.

Bainbridge was a large, pompous man, lacking much in the way of wit
or imagination, but a competent officer for all that. He had won his laurels

in the War of 1812 by capturing the British frigate *Java* off the coast of Brazil when in command of the *Constitution*. But that victory had not wiped away the shame connected with his previous visits to the Mediterranean, when the dey of Algiers had first used him as an errand boy, and later, the bashaw of Tripoli had captured his ship and held him prisoner for two years. Those two humiliating incidents had engendered in him a fierce determination to avenge himself against his oppressors. He had been gratified by the American declaration of war against Algiers, and thrilled to learn he would command a squadron that would bring the dey to terms. He was convinced he had earned the right, both by seniority and as a result of the indignities that had been heaped upon him by a cruel history, to lead the fight against the Barbary states.

Bainbridge had only learned at a later date that the squadron would be divided into two sections, and that Decatur would lead the first. The news was admittedly troubling, but he took comfort in the fact that Decatur had expressed his determination to return home as soon as the two squadrons met, and Bainbridge was confident that when the negotiations got serious, he alone would remain as commander-in-chief, and reap the kudos for the anticipated diplomatic triumph.

With his mind filled with such dreams of glory, it came as a devastating blow to learn from a passing ship on the day after his arrival in the Mediterranean that Decatur had already won a naval battle with the Algerines, after which he had sailed to Algiers and forced the dey to accept American terms for peace. Singlehandedly Decatur had already accomplished the most important object of the entire expedition. Bainbridge was crushed. He fell deathly ill at the news and was confined to his cabin for a full week.

By September Decatur was well aware of Bainbridge's arrival in the Mediterranean but had made no great efforts to find him. By the middle of the month, he decided it was time to turn over his command and sail home. He sent the other vessels in his squadron off to Malaga, where he expected they would find Bainbridge. A few days later, sailing alone in the *Guerriere,* he was bound on a westerly course to join them.

If Decatur was feeling a sense of satisfaction at that point he cannot be faulted. He had earned his success. In less than three months, he had crossed the ocean, forced three hostile powers to sue for peace, and in one glorious confrontation after another had eclipsed all the heroics of his earlier exploits. He wrote home: "I trust that the successful result of our small expedition, so honorable to our country, will induce other nations to follow the example; in which case the Barbary states will be compelled to abandon their piratical system." If the loss of the *President* in January 1815 marked the nadir of his lifelong pursuit of glory, the triumphs of the following summer marked the resounding apogee. It was, by his own estimation, the crowning achievement of his remarkable career.

As the *Guerriere* beat down the Mediterranean against a moderate westerly breeze, a call from a lookout announced a squadron of seven warships standing to the northward, heading in their direction under easy sail. Decatur went below and changed into his uniform before returning to the quarterdeck to await the approaching squadron. The strangers, being on the opposite tack, advanced rapidly, and soon showed themselves to be Algerines. There were four frigates and three sloops. Decatur was vastly outnumbered. He had to consider the possibility that the Algerines, finding him alone, might choose to break the new treaty and take the *Guerriere* in prize in retaliation for the *Mashouda.* While such a rash move was unlikely, he could not dismiss the possibility. He ordered the drummer to beat to quarters and cleared the decks for action.

The Algerines came on in line of battle, the ship bearing the admiral, distinguished by his personal flag, bringing up the rear. One by one they passed to leeward in silence, until the flagship came alongside. The admiral stood in the gangway with a speaking trumpet and using the Italian patois that was the common language of the western Mediterranean, shouted over to Decatur, *"Dove andante?"* that is, "Where are you bound?"

The courtesy of the sea required that when ships of war approached each other in times of peace with colors displayed, the ship that left her course to speak out to another should first state her name before addressing the other vessel. Decatur, irritated by the Algerine's breach of manners, took the speaking trumpet from the officer of the deck and shouted back, *"Dove mi piace!"* meaning "I go where I please!"

The moment seemed to encapsulate the entire summer—the pride, the zeal, the truculence of a man in charge, enjoying every minute of it. The Algerines made no further response, and continued on their way.

On October 7, a sullen and embittered William Bainbridge prepared to take his huge flotilla home. In the Bay of Gibraltar, under his sole command, lay both parts of the Mediterranean squadron, by far the largest American fleet ever assembled, seventeen sail in all, including his flagship, the seventy-four-gun *Independence,* four frigates, and assorted brigs, sloops of war, and schooners. The only vessel missing was the *Guerriere.* It was a magnificent armada, and its size and power should have been enough to make any commodore's breast swell with pride. But the command of such a glorious assembly of ships was little more than a hollow honor to William Bainbridge. He had expected that the cruise would provide a capstone to his career. Instead, due entirely to Stephen Decatur, who had elbowed his way into the assignment and deliberately worked against Bainbridge's interests in order to burnish his own reputation, Bainbridge's moment of triumph had been reduced to a deeply disappointing exercise in frustration and futility.

After learning of Decatur's success at Algiers, Bainbridge had been left with the decidedly subordinate role of leading his squadron to the same city and showing the flag. He had then moved on to Tunis and Tripoli, only to find that in both instances he had again been preceded by Decatur. For all its size and power, Bainbridge's squadron had proved to be totally irrelevant. The commodore was acutely aware that his whole squadron was witness to his embarrassment, and he could imagine that his own officers were quietly enjoying his discomforture. It was intolerable.

Perhaps the only saving grace was Decatur's personal absence. He had dutifully sent his ships forward to join Bainbridge's squadron, but so far he had not appeared himself. But if Bainbridge had hopes of avoiding Decatur altogether, he was again to be disappointed. As the *Independence* made her way out of the harbor with her magnificent squadron in attendance, the *Guerriere* was seen to heave into sight around Europa Point and stand in toward the bay. The entire squadron, thrilled by the dramatic appearance of the great Decatur, broke into cheers.

The *Guerriere* hove to as she approached the stern of the *Independence* and paid the customary salute of honor to the flag of the commander-in-chief. The salute was duly returned, but the *Independence* made no attempt to slow her own passage. Decatur, resplendent in full uniform, climbed into a waiting gig, which had his commodore's pennant at her bow. The oarsmen pulled hard toward the *Independence,* which held her course and was clearly trying to avoid a meeting. Eventually, Decatur managed to catch up and climb on board.

There is no record of what transpired in the meeting of the two commodores on board the *Independence* that day, other than an account given by Susan Decatur many years later, based on what her husband had told her.

"When my husband went on board on a very tempestuous day to pay his respects . . . [Bainbridge] received him as a *total stranger!*—never asked a single question relative to our affairs! and never offered him the slightest hospitality! This is the person who had frequently been our guest for weeks at a time! and declaring that he loved my husband as much as he did his own wife and children."

Very soon after his arrival, Decatur was seen to return to his gig and to the *Guerriere*. He could have taken no pleasure in the bitter meeting he had just attended. Nothing in Decatur's life suggests a meanness or arrogance in his character. It seems likely that the intensity of Bainbridge's fury came as a surprise. It had simply never occurred to Decatur that his own ruthless pursuit of glory, and his determination to make up for the loss of the *Presi-*

dent had consequences that were extremely painful to a man of Bainbridge's history and nature.

If Decatur had indeed regained his honor, he had paid a high price, and had made for himself a bitter enemy for what was to be the brief remainder of his life.

SIXTEEN

The Navy Board

Decatur brought the *Guerriere* into New York on November 12, 1815. His return was greeted by ecstatic jubilation, and any anxieties he may have harbored about his popularity as a result of the loss of the *President* were banished for good. Once again he was the nation's most revered naval figure. His public still adored him, and for several days he held the national stage alone, until Bainbridge and the rest of the squadron made it into Newport later in the week.

Praise radiated from the highest levels. Secretary of State James Monroe wrote to tell him that "this expedition, so glorious to your country and honorable to yourself and the officers and men under your command, has been very satisfactory to the President."

David Porter, a comrade in arms from the Tripoli wars, wrote from Washington to congratulate him on "your safe and speedy return from your brilliant comet-like expedition to our old friends. You have done more in a few months than all Europe have been able to effect in ages, and have given a lesson not only to Christendom but to the Barbary States that will not soon be forgotten."

The press was equally laudatory, and President Madison accorded him a signal honor by singling him out for special praise in the opening paragraphs of his annual message to Congress—the equivalent of the present State of the Union address—crediting him alone for bringing the dey of Algiers to heel.

Decatur left New York as soon as possible for Philadelphia and Susan, and while in that city received a letter from Secretary of the Navy Crownin-

shield celebrating his triumphs and offering him a seat on the prestigious
Board of Navy Commissioners, the recently instituted three-man commission that served much the same function as the Lords of the Admiralty in
the British navy. It was the highest office open to a uniformed naval officer
and carried with it an annual salary of thirty-five hundred dollars, almost
double the amount he drew in the form of base pay and allotments. Prestigious shore duty was exactly what Susan had wished for, and he was
quick to accept.

On the way south to Washington he was given a gala dinner by the
city fathers of Baltimore. Guests included every naval officer who could
be found in the area, plus many army officers and members of Congress.
Toward the end of the dinner, the festivities were given over to toasts,
"with glees accompanied by appropriate music from Mr. Bunye's band."

One of the first toasts was, "Algiers, and the other Barbary powers!
Taught by Decatur's gallant squadron to respect the laws of nations!"
Decatur's response recalled the defense of his host city when it was attacked
by the British in 1814. "The citizens of Baltimore! Their patriotism and
valor defeated the veteran forces of their enemy, who came, saw and fled!"

There was much cheering and revelry, right up to the closing toast,
given by the chairman of the affair: "Commodore Decatur! The man
whom his country delights to honor!"

The embryonic capital of Washington was still more of a grandiose idea
than a true city at the time of the Decaturs' arrival. It had been laid out on
an Olympian scale by Pierre Charles L'Enfant, the French city planner, to
represent "the genius of the new republic." The widely spread out public
buildings, many of them still unfinished, were often isolated and difficult
to reach. Large stretches of Pennsylvania Avenue, the main thoroughfare,
were almost impassable with tangles of elder bushes, swamp grass, and
tree stumps. One visitor tried to put as good a face as possible on the pre-
tentious and inherently awkward design of Washington by calling it "the
city of magnificent distances."

Soon after their arrival the Decaturs purchased one of the "Seven Buildings," a centrally located group of expensive attached houses on Pennsylvania Avenue between Nineteenth and Twentieth Streets. Their next door neighbor, in the largest of the seven, was President James Madison, who had been forced to move out of the Presidential Mansion temporarily after it was gutted by the British in the war.

The offices of the Navy Board were nearby. The duties of the three commissioners, Commodores John Rodgers, David Porter, and Stephen Decatur, were broad and varied. They determined what kind of ships the navy should build, and what construction standards should apply; they organized recruitment and established the numbers and ranks of officers; they were responsible for the purchase and storage of naval supplies, including timber, guns, food, ship chandlery, and whiskey, and worked for the improvement of training and equipment.

Decatur did not take naturally to the very different world of bureaucracy, where life was more complicated and relationships more nuanced. He was neither by nature nor inclination an administrator, and his blunt shipboard manner had a tendency to cause friction. Once, when his fellow commissioner David Porter objected to his interference, Decatur jumped to his feet and said hotly, "Exactly, sir! Since you and Commodore Rodgers always vote against me, I am of little use here!"

Porter responded sharply, "That sir—to say the best of it—is untrue! Your complaint is frivolous, and for what I say I hold myself responsible!"

Both of these hotheaded autocrats, accustomed to their unquestioned authority on the quarterdeck, stormed off, but were soon back on friendly terms.

Decatur was now thirty-seven years old, no longer youthful, but not yet fully seasoned. His close interaction with diplomats and statesmen in the Mediterranean, and particularly his success at negotiating peace with the Barbary states, had taught him something about the use of arms to achieve one's goals—that the threat of action could at times be even more productive than action itself, and that for a man still ambitious to improve himself and his place in the world there might be new skills worth learning. He was bringing to the process of maturing the same quick mind and dogged determination that had served him in his youth.

He did not lack for qualified teachers. William Rush, his old schoolmate and the attorney general in Madison's cabinet, remembered how, during those early years in Washington, Decatur and President Madison had established strong personal ties. "Mr. Madison . . . was impressed with the enlargement of [Decatur's] views and conversation, and, above all, his enlightened thirst for correct knowledge of the true elements of our constitutional government."

Madison, generally credited as the "father of the Constitution," and the principal author of the anonymous *Federalist Papers* published in support of its ratification, took a personal hand in Decatur's education. "In this connection," Rush recalled, "it is also known to me, that Mr. Madison kindly designated, with his own pencil or pen, in the copy of the Federalist, which the Commodore was reading, the numbers of that great work written by General Hamilton, Mr. Jay, or himself."

Such tutelage could not help but have an effect. Decatur grew increasingly thoughtful. Richard Rush remembered an instance when Decatur displayed his knowledge of naval history, his skeptical assessment of the French navy, and his less than worshipful analysis of the great Nelson's strategy at Trafalgar:

> *One day when he was dining with me in Washington with a few other naval officers, the conversation after dinner turned upon the naval history and battles of England. He remarked that he thought England would change her mode of fighting in large fleets, if ever she encountered a skillful enemy fleet to fleet. To sustain this position, he analyzed the battle of Trafalgar; and whilst enthusiastically admiring Nelson's heroism, said that he, nevertheless, owed that victory to the extraordinary deficiency of the French and Spaniards in their naval*

gunnery, alleging that, if it had been quick and true on that occasion, the English ships must have been crippled more or less, and some of them cut to pieces while in the very act of breaking the enemy's line. He gave his illustrations with nutshells on the table, arranged to show the relative positions and maneuvering of the two fleets; and I remember his dwelling with emphasis on the vital importance of gunnery in naval discipline and practice, saying that everything else went for nothing at all (as must be obvious) without it, unless you mean to fight only by boarding; and that to make it perfect, the men must not only be laboriously exercised at the guns in rough as well as smooth weather, but with ball cartridge at the target, rising and falling in the water.

The topic called up Rodney's action with De Grasse, towards the close of our revolutionary war, on which occasion Rodney's leading ship, the Marlborough, *received the successive broadsides of more than twenty of the French ships of the line, and this at near distance, without losing more than half a dozen of her men, or sustaining any material damage. Could naval firing, he asked, be more wild? and declared that, if the guns of the French fleet had been well served, the* Marlborough *must have been destroyed. It was plain that he had no opinion of breaking the line as a mode of attack, unless you were full sure of your enemy's defects in seamanship and gunnery.*

Stephen and Susan fitted in comfortably with Washington's movers and shakers. His heroic exploits, high office, and prize money sufficient to finance a good table, combined with her sparkling intellect, musical skills, and practiced charm, gave them a glamorous presence and helped them cut a considerable swath. An indication of his renown can be found in the elegant simplicity of his personal calling card. There was no need to list either his rank, address, or even his full name. The design consisted simply of a small illustration of the *United States* battling the *Macedonian,* surmounted discreetly by his surname alone:

The United States and Macedonian

Along with their social prominence came a highly agreeable dash of power and influence. Decatur played an important part in convincing a reluctant Congress to support a permanent navy, and in April 1816 it authorized the construction of nine ships of the line and twelve large frigates. They would be used to help protect and expand American interests overseas—forming the foundation of America's international presence. Gone forever was the gunboat navy.

Another indication of his growing influence in Washington was the speed with which Congress voted to award one hundred thousand dollars in prize money for the two ships Decatur had captured from the Algerines, and later returned to the dey. Decatur's share came to fifteen thousand dollars, bestowed by a grateful Congress that had steadfastly refused to authorize the payment of one dime for the destruction of the *Philadelphia*.

Public adulation continued. In April 1816, at an "entertainment" given in his honor at Norfolk, Decatur was serenaded with a song specially written for the occasion. The lyrics were set to a standard melody popular at the time, called "To Anacreon in Heaven," which happened to be the same piece of music that Francis Scott Key had recently used to accompany a patriotic anthem he called "The Star Spangled Banner."

DECATUR, VICTOR OVER ALGIERS

See Decatur, our hero, returns to the West,
Who's destined to shine in the annals of story,
A bright ray of victory beams high on his crest;
Encircled, his brows by a halo of glory.
On Afric's bleak shore,
From the insolent Moor,
His bloody, stained laurels in triumph he tore,
Where the Crescent *which oft spread its terrors afar*
Submissively bowed to the American Star.

Algiers' haughty Dey in the height of his pride
From American freemen a tribute demanded;
Columbia's brave freemen a tribute denied,
And his corsairs to seize our bold tars were commanded.
Their streamers wave high,
But Decatur *draws nigh;*
His name strikes like lightning—in terror they fly.
Thrice welcome, our hero, returned from afar,
Where the proud Crescent *falls to the American* Star.

Accompanying the song were numerous toasts, including many that resounded with patriotic fervor, such as: "The Mediterranean—the sea not more of Greek and Roman than of American glory," and "National Glory—a gem above all price, and worthy every hazard to sustain its splendor." As the night wore on, the party took on a somewhat raucous character as each speaker, after delivering his toast, drained his wine glass and tossed it over his shoulder. When Decatur's turn came, he responded with what were to become his most famous words, "Our Country! In her intercourse with foreign nations may she always be in the *right*, and *always successful, right or wrong!*" Then, swept up in the high spirits of the moment, he threw away his glass with such cheerful abandon that it shattered a mirror behind him, to the cheers and delight of all those present.

After a similar testimonial given to Decatur a few days later in Petersburg, Virginia, the editor of *Niles' Weekly Register* wondered, "How must a man feel thus to receive the caresses of a whole people!"

The Decaturs had no children, but were often host to his sister's three daughters. Their father, Captain McKnight of the Marine Corps, had been killed in a duel in 1802, and Decatur served as his surrogate. By all accounts, he was a loving and thoughtful mentor. Maintaining a busy household and active social life required domestic help, which in Washington, a distinctly southern town, almost always meant slaves. As far as can be ascertained the Decaturs owned no slaves but may well have rented them from others, a practice that suggests a certain ambivalence relating to the South's peculiar institution.

By 1817, the Decaturs' circumstances had improved to the point that they decided to build a permanent home in Washington. They purchased a lot on H Street near the Presidential Mansion, now fully restored and occupied by the newly elected James Monroe. Their new home, designed by Benjamin H. Latrobe, the architect of the Capitol Building, would announce to the world that its owners had indeed arrived, and would now take their permanent place among the powerful and influential, at the very heart of the nation. Decatur House remains a prominent Washington landmark to this day.

Across the seas in London, another American naval officer was also looking toward the future. Although his plans were far more modest than those of Stephen and Susan Decatur, they would eventually affect the glamorous couple in a devastating manner. More than ten years after his suspension from the navy for his part in the *Chesapeake–Leopard* Affair, Commodore James Barron was coming home.

SEVENTEEN

Barron Returns

The United States Navy, like any community made up of fractious, high-spirited individuals jealous of their prerogatives and prone to belligerent reaction to any perceived slight, was bound to boil over occasionally with differences of opinion that led to bitter feuds and enmities. Within the officer corps, at any given time, there always seemed to be four or five apparently irreconcilable misunderstandings that could be settled only by trial by combat, or as it was euphemistically described, "a call to the field of honor."

Stephen Decatur had initiated at least one such call when still a very junior lieutenant, but he had long since outgrown any interest in dueling, and over the years his "Decatur Plan" had in fact contributed significantly to the decline of the practice, at least among hot-blooded midshipmen. But not every officer was interested in following Decatur's lead.

One of the most thin-skinned and pugnacious captains in the early navy was his friend Commodore Oliver Hazard Perry, the hero of the Battle of Lake Erie. In 1818 Perry was involved in not one, but two different feuds serious enough to have generated a call to the field. The first was with Marine Captain John Heath, whom Perry had struck in a fit of temper when in command of the frigate *Java*. When Heath refused to accept Perry's apology, the only recourse was a duel.

Perry's other feud, a more complicated matter, was with a troublesome officer and mischief maker named Jesse Duncan Elliott, who had been his second in command at Lake Erie. Long after the battle, Perry had publicly accused Elliott of deliberately avoiding action in that engagement, and when Elliott denounced Perry's claims as slander and challenged him to a duel, Perry disdainfully refused, claiming Elliott was no gentleman, and it was therefore beneath his dignity to accept such a challenge. He would honor such a call to the field, he told Elliott, only if a court-martial cleared him of Perry's charges.

Stephen Decatur was probably Perry's closest friend, and in October 1818, he traveled to New York to serve as Perry's second in his long-postponed meeting with Captain Heath. The duel took place across the Hudson, in Hoboken. Perry deliberately fired into the ground and Heath just as deliberately shot wide, missing his opponent on purpose. Both parties agreed that their honor had been upheld, and the matter was closed.

It was probably at this meeting between the two friends that Decatur, as spokesman for the Board of Navy Commissioners, explained to Perry the government's reluctance to convene a court-martial to look into his charges against his other enemy, Jesse Elliott. Perry's case against Elliott was equivocal, Decatur explained, and the board thought it best to postpone such a court until some later time. While the unresolved question of Jesse Elliott's alleged improprieties on Lake Erie had no direct ties to Decatur, they would in time become an important thread in the complicated tapestry of events that would lead to the meeting at Bladensburg.

In December 1818, two months after the duel between Perry and Heath in Hoboken, Commodore James Barron finally arrived back in America. He had been out of the country for six years, having spent almost all of that time in Copenhagen. His voyage from Liverpool had been long and circuitous, and Barron, now fifty years old and flat broke, was so anxious to apply for reinstatement that he went directly to the Navy Department, even before returning to his family in Hampton, Virginia.

His years in Copenhagen had been a sad and dispiriting time for Barron. He had tried to make a living as a merchant skipper, and when that did not work out, as an inventor of nautical machines—he had taken out a number of Danish patents—but it had been a hand to mouth existence, and he had been compelled to depend largely on the kindness of friends to make ends meet. Meanwhile, his wife and daughters in Virginia made do as best they could on the fifty dollars a month half pay they had received from the navy ever since his five-year suspension came to an end in 1813.

Barron arrived at the Navy Department at an awkward time. When he presented himself at the office of the secretary of the navy, he learned from a clerk named Benjamin Homans that there was no one holding that job at the time, and that if he wished to speak to someone in authority he would have to see one of the three commissioners of the Navy Board. When Barron learned that the three commissioners were Commodores Rodgers, Porter, and Decatur, all of whom had sat on the court-martial that suspended him for his part in the *Leopard–Chesapeake* incident, he decided to postpone his application for reinstatement until another time.

The clerk was friendly, and seemed to have a good grasp of who Barron was, and the circumstances surrounding his case. Barron asked him if he had any idea why his request for duty, which he had written from Copenhagen in 1813, had not been answered, or why he had received no subsequent orders in all the years since his suspension ended. Homans suggested that the previous navy secretaries may have been influenced by a letter that had been received by the department several years previously, implicating Barron in purported improprieties at Pernambuco, in Brazil.

Barron was puzzled to learn of such a letter. He had no idea what it might contain, or how it could have caused such a drastic reaction. But it was pointless to protest to a departmental clerk. Very much shaken by his visit, he booked passage on the steam packet to Hampton Roads, where he would be reunited with his family and where he hoped to find some way to overcome his difficulties. Over the next several weeks, Barron began planning a campaign to return him to active duty. He would need friends in high places to help him. He remained on good terms with many of the members of Virginia's congressional delegation, and they agreed to support his efforts for reinstatement. From old navy comrades he learned details of what had been happening at home over the years of his ostracism. He was particularly interested to hear of the travails of Captain Jesse Duncan Elliott. Barron had a particular interest in Elliott, who had been a midshipman in the *Chesapeake* at the time of the attack by the *Leop-*

ard, and who had been virtually the only witness in Barron's court-martial who had stood up for his commander. Barron made a special trip to Baltimore to learn of Elliott's subsequent history at first hand.

The two men were very different in character and outlook, but Barron, as a result of his court-martial conviction, and Elliott, because of his very public feud with Perry, were both pariahs within the officer corps, and the two outsiders had a natural reason to find common cause. The fact that Elliott's enemy happened to be a particularly close friend of Decatur would have undoubtedly helped create a further bond between the two men.

To this day, Jesse Duncan Elliott remains something of an enigma. He has been called the stormy petrel of the American navy, and there is no question he thrived on controversy. He was apparently a good enough officer, but he was also devious, argumentative, and a natural-born troublemaker. There was in his character a contrarian streak that seemed to constantly land him in difficulties of one kind or another. The friendship that grew up between the contentious Elliott and the cautious, thoughtful Barron was a relationship of opposites, built more on a commonality of enemies than any sympathy of spirit.

By February 1819, President Monroe had finally settled on Smith Thompson as his new secretary of the navy, and Barron prepared to approach him and formally apply for reinstatement. He wrote to Thompson and also to the president—a fellow Virginian—informing them that he had learned of a hostile letter in the departmental files, and that he would welcome an investigation. He then took the packet north to pursue his campaign in Washington.

His meeting with Secretary Thompson was correct but cool. Thompson sent for the letter that Barron had referred to and handed it over to him. As Barron read it, he grew increasingly incredulous. For the first time he learned the details of William Lewis's damning account of the comments supposedly made by Barron to the British consul in Pernambuco, including the commodore's determination not to resist the *Leopard*'s attack and his purported accusation that President Jefferson had deliberately wanted to create an international incident.

Barron finished reading the letter, and very much taken aback, returned it to Thompson. He assured the secretary that there was not a shred of truth to it, that it was all some sort of gross misunderstanding, and that he would immediately take all necessary steps to prove his innocence. Thompson responded that unfortunately the writer of the letter had been lost at sea in 1815 and could not bear witness to the circumstances that had led him to write it.

Captain Lewis's letter was serious enough, but Secretary Thompson let him know there were further obstacles to his reinstatement. It had been averred by unnamed sources that during the late war with Britain Barron had served as master of a merchantman sailing under British license. If the story was true, it was an even more grave matter than the Pernambuco letter, for such an act was treason. Even if he could disprove the story, there was the related question of why he had not returned to fight in the war when his suspension came to an end. These were all serious matters, Thompson told him, and before any consideration could be given to his application, Barron would have to provide explanations. For the first time, Barron saw exactly where he stood. He was confident that he could clear himself, but it would obviously require time and effort.

On leaving the secretary's office, Barron recognized a familiar figure walking toward him. It was Commodore John Rodgers, president of the Navy Board. Although the two men had had their differences in the past, Barron was determined to put such matters behind him and made it a point to raise his hat to Rodgers as they passed. Rodgers took no notice of Barron and walked on as if he were not there. The deliberate snub—the cut direct, as it was known—made it clear to Barron that he had more to worry about than simply disproving stories about his past.

Barron's reappearance in Washington after ten years created a stir in navy circles. The story of his bid for reinstatement quickly became a major topic among his former peers, and a matter of considerable interest even to those who had never known him.

Decatur's reaction to the news was immediate and unequivocal. No matter what the circumstances, he was totally against Barron's reinstatement. He had nothing in particular against the man, he explained. He had in times past enjoyed his company. He admired his seamanship. He recalled how Barron, in a hurricane all those many years before off Cape Hatteras, had personally, and at great risk to himself, saved the frigate *United States* and all the men on board. In a very real sense, Decatur knew he probably owed his life to James Barron. But that did not alter his opinion of his fitness as an officer. It was a naval officer's first duty to fight, not to sail ships. Back in 1807, when he tried to excuse himself from serving on Barron's court-martial panel, he had stated frankly that his "opinion of him as a soldier was not favorable."

Decatur would have had no quarrel if Barron had been willing to return to the navy as a sailing master—responsible solely for the maintenance and handling of the ship—but such a possibility was unthinkable. For a man holding the highest rank in the navy to submit to such an ignominious demotion was not to be imagined.

But the question of Barron's right to return to active duty could not be brushed aside. He had served his sentence—a sentence that some thought unfair—and it was quite proper for him to seek reinstatement. But to Decatur—and those who thought as he did—there was more to the question than a matter of individual rights. There was the navy itself to consider. The service had changed significantly since the *Leopard–Chesapeake* incident—a change that had been brought about in part by the incident itself. The navy had been held up to ridicule and public shame and compelled to fight to regain its honor. As a result of the great catharsis it had undergone, it had won glory in the war, and now stood at the height of public esteem. It was run by men who had tested themselves in the fires of combat, men who had earned their right to command. Now those men were training the next generation. There was no place in such an elite service for a man who had struck his colors without a fight.

Decatur was outspoken in his determination to oppose Barron's return to the service. Most of his fellow officers agreed with him, but few could match his passion or his eloquence. He spoke out frankly and often, and everyone knew where he stood on the question.

Barron fought back as best he could. True to their word, a number of Virginia congressmen drew up a memorial supporting his return to active duty and sent it to the president. The combative Jesse Duncan Elliott was also active on behalf of his former commander. He came to Washington and personally lobbied the secretary of the navy, but Smith Thompson, after listening patiently to Elliott's impassioned arguments, informed him coolly that he was the only man on the captains list who desired Barron's reinstatement and pointedly reminded him that his name stood at the bottom of that list.

In the spring of 1819, while Barron awaited the letters from Copenhagen and Pernambuco that he hoped would put the lie to the charge that he had sailed under British license, and disprove William Lewis's damning letter, a new face showed up in Washington—that of Oliver Hazard Perry. President Monroe was sending him to South America to negotiate some matters with Simon Bolívar, and while he awaited sailing orders Perry enjoyed the hospitality of Stephen and Susan Decatur in their elegant new home.

Perry was well aware of the dangers inherent in his trip to South America. Given the hazardous political situation and the ever-present threat of tropical diseases, it was always possible that he might not return, in which case his feud with Elliott might well be forgotten or ignored. He asked Decatur to take care of his papers, which he claimed documented his charges against Elliott. If he failed to return, he wanted Decatur to make them public. Susan Decatur recalled the discussion between the two commodores many years later: "Perry remarked to my husband that Elliott was so regardless of truth and every principle of honor that there was no knowing what he might say if there were no person to keep him in check! . . . So soon as Perry left the room, I observed to my husband that as Elliott was considered so destitute of principle, I was afraid he [i.e., Decatur] might get himself into some difficulty. He replied that it was his duty to watch over the reputation of his brother officers; and that I need not make myself uneasy, that Elliott was too great a coward to approach him in any way, and he did not believe there was an officer in the navy whom he could make use of as a cat's paw."

Meanwhile, at his home in Hampton, James Barron heard a report of some disparaging comments that Decatur had let drop during a recent tour of the nearby Norfolk Navy Yard. Barron had chosen to ignore similar reports from friends in Washington, but he felt he could not overlook such an attack when it occurred so close to home. He decided to face the issue directly, and wrote Decatur a brief but dignified letter.

HAMPTON, VA. June 12, 1819

Sir—I have been informed in Norfolk that you have said that you could insult me with impunity, or words to that effect. If you have said so, no doubt you will avow it, and I shall expect to hear from you.
I am, sir, your obedient servant,
JAMES BARRON

To Commodore STEPHEN DECATUR,
Washington

EIGHTEEN

The Challenge

Decatur could not have been overly surprised by Barron's angry note. He had spoken openly of his disapproval of his former commander, both publicly and at his own table, and he could only assume that the time would come when he would be called to account for it. Nor would he have been shy about stating the reasons for his opinion, had Barron requested as much. But Barron had not. Instead, he had raised the issue of an alleged insult, and done so in what seemed to Decatur a muddled, confused manner ill-suited to such an important subject.

Decatur, always the fighter, opened his response with an attack:

> *SIR: I have received your communication. . . . Before you could have been entitled to the information you have asked of me, you should have given up the name of your informer. That frankness which ought to characterise our profession required it.*

Having made his point, he proceeded to answer Barron's question in a forceful yet curiously circuitous manner:

> *I shall not, however, refuse to answer you on that account, but shall be as candid in my communication to you as your letter or the case will warrant.*
> *Whatever I may have <u>thought, or said, in the very frequent and free conversations I have had respecting you and your conduct,</u> I feel a thorough conviction that I never could have been guilty of so much egotism as to say that "<u>I</u> could insult you" (or any other man) "with impunity."*
> *I am, sir, your obedient servant,*
> *STEPHEN DECATUR*

The answer, with its dramatic underlinings, openly admitted speaking often and publicly against Barron, but made the point that he had not made the specific derogatory claim cited in Barron's letter.

Decatur's aggressive tone proved effective. Barron's response was that of a man scrambling to regain the high moral ground. He acknowledged his breech of etiquette in not naming his informant (whom he again failed to identify), and then closed with a dignified withdrawal of his charge:

> *Your declaration, if I understand it correctly, relieves my mind from the apprehension that you had so degraded my character, as I had been induced to allege.*
>
>

I am, sir, your obedient servant,
JAMES BARRON

There the correspondence should have ended, and almost certainly would have, had Decatur been willing to leave well enough alone. But instead he felt constrained to respond one more time, in a letter that would make it easy for Barron to eventually reignite the controversy and lead to a lengthy exchange of contentious letters that would continue into the following year. Decatur's second letter to Barron has been characterized as "not far short of insulting," but that is almost certainly overstating the case. Decatur was not a vindictive man. He displayed a short temper at times, and perhaps an overly simplistic sense of right and wrong, but he was not a bully, nor a man with a desire to humiliate. It is probably more accurate to see Decatur's second letter as his earnest attempt to explain just how strongly he opposed Barron's return to active duty, and his determination to oppose it.

> *SIR: I have received your communication of the 25th, in answer to mine of the 17th, and, as you have expressed yourself doubtfully, as to your correct understanding of my letter of the aforesaid date, I have now to state, and I request you to understand distinctly, that I meant no more than to*

disclaim the <u>specific</u> and <u>particular</u> expression to which your inquiry was directed, to wit: that I had said that <u>I</u> could insult you with impunity. . . .

Your obedient servant,

STEPHEN DECATUR

Barron did not immediately respond. There was no need to. But there was bound to be continued friction between the two because Barron was still determined to return to the navy, and Decatur was equally determined to thwart him. Throughout the summer of 1819, each pursued his own course of action, Decatur devoting himself to his duties at the Navy Board, Barron continuing his lobbying efforts with his friends in Congress.

Then in September word reached America from Venezuela of the death by yellow fever of Commodore Oliver Hazard Perry. While the news would have had no particular significance to James Barron, it would have been of singular interest to Captain Jesse Duncan Elliott. Elliott was well aware of the damning affidavits and other evidence against him that Perry had collected, and the threat they posed to his career. News of Perry's death would have relieved him of considerable worries. But Elliott almost certainly knew, or guessed, that Perry had left those damning papers in the care of Stephen Decatur, and therefore the threat still remained. Given the circumstances, Perry's death did not so much relieve Elliott's anxieties as cause him to transfer his animosity to Decatur. It was now in Elliott's immediate interest to discredit Decatur by any means available.

A scandalous duel might well fill the bill.

Elliott and Barron, the two outsiders, had by now established a close relationship, and almost certainly it was Elliott who persuaded Barron to reopen his correspondence with Decatur after four months of silence. On October 23, 1819, Barron sent a letter to Decatur that was markedly different in tone and style from the two previous ones. It was a long, rambling, and often confused list of complaints, quite obviously designed to provoke a fight. Proof of Elliott's complicity in this and subsequent letters is circumstantial, but there is no question there is a very different quality to the writing, which is quarrelsome and at times self-pitying and envious, lacking much of the inherent dignity of his earlier letters.

> *SIR: I had supposed that the measure of your ambition was nearly completed, and that your good fortune had rendered your reputation for acts of magnanimity too dear to be risked wantonly on occasions that can never redound to the honor of him that would be great. I had also concluded that your rancor towards me was fully satisfied, by the cruel and unmerited sentence passed upon me by the court of which you were a member; and, after an exile from my country, family, and friends, of nearly seven years, I had concluded that I should now be allowed, at least, to enjoy that solace, with this society, that lacerated feelings like mine required, and that you would have suffered me to remain in quiet possession of those enjoyments; but, scarcely had I set my foot on my native soil, ere I learnt that the same malignant spirit which had before influenced you to endeavor to ruin my reputation was still at work, and that you were ungenerously traducing my character whenever an occasion occurred which suited your views. . . .*

Barron alludes directly, for the first time, to the subject of dueling:

> *I am also informed that you have tauntingly and boastingly observed, that you would cheerfully meet me in the field, and hoped that I would yet act like a man, or that you had used words to that effect; such conduct, on the part of any one, but especially one occupying the influential station under the government which you hold, towards an individual, situated as I am, and oppressed as I have been, and that chiefly by your means, is unbecoming you as an officer and gentleman; and shews a want of magnimity which, hostile as I have found you to be towards me, I had hoped for your own reputation you possessed.*

By such tortured reasoning Barron then claimed that Decatur had, through his hostile comments, already challenged him, and he therefore claimed the right of the challenged party to set the terms of the fight.

I consider you as having given the invitation, which I accept, and will
prepare to meet you at such time and place as our respective friends,
hereafter to be named, shall designate. I also, under all the circumstances
of the case, consider myself entitled to the choice of weapons, place, and
distance. . . .

I am, sir, your obedient servant,
JAMES BARRON

Of course Decatur had not challenged Barron, nor did he intend to do so. It is unlikely that either Barron or Elliott expected Decatur to accept such a flimsy version of events. The probable intent was simply to provoke him, and in this they succeeded.

Decatur was well aware of the connection between Barron and Elliott. A private letter to Decatur, filled with blank spaces in place of proper names, but with the names easily identifiable from the context, throws considerable light on the situation. The letter was written by his friend and advisor, the Norfolk lawyer Littleton Tazewell. "But one opinion exists with all the Naval Officers here . . ." Tazewell reported, "that [Elliott] is the sole instigator of the renewal of the correspondence, and has done everything in his power to stimulate his reluctant friend. . . . That [Barron] would gladly now let the thing rest *if he can,* but that [Elliott] will prevent any sort of adjustment if he can do so."

A week after Barron had reopened the correspondence, Decatur answered him in an extremely long, exasperated letter of almost twenty-five hundred words, answering point by point each of Barron's complaints.

SIR: Your letter of the 23rd inst. has been duly received. . . . Between
you and myself, there never has been a personal difference; but I have
entertained, and do still entertain the opinion, that your conduct as an
officer, since the affair of the <u>Chesapeake,</u> has been such as ought to for-
ever bar your re-admission into the service. . . . In the many and <u>free</u> con-
versations I have had respecting you and your conduct, I have said . . .

that, in my opinion, you ought not to be received again into the naval ser-
vice; that there was not employment for all the officers who had faithfully
discharged their duty to their country in the hour of trial; and that it
would be doing an act of injustice to employ you, to the exclusion of any
one of them. In speaking thus, and endeavouring to prevent your re-
admission, I conceive that I was performing a duty I owe to the service;
that I was contributing to the preservation of its respectability.

He made the point that his negative opinion of Barron's fitness was widely held in the officer corps, and included a veiled but deliberate swipe at Elliott:

. . . I can assure you, that, in the interchange of opinions with other offi-
cers respecting you, I have never met with more than one who did not
entirely concur with me.

Toward the end of his letter, Decatur dismissed Barron's lame assertion that Decatur had already challenged him.

You profess to consider me as having given you "an invitation." . . . I
never invited you to the field; nor have I expressed a hope that you would
call me out . . . if you made the call, I would meet you; but . . . I should be
much better pleased, to have nothing to do with you.

He closed with an eloquent condemnation of dueling.

I do not think that fighting duels, under any circumstances, can raise the
reputation of any man, and have long since discovered, that it is not even
an unerring criterion of personal courage. I should regret the necessity of
fighting with any man; but, in my opinion, the man who makes <u>arms his</u>
<u>profession,</u> is not at liberty to decline an invitation. . . .

I am, sir, your obedient servant,
STEPHEN DECATUR

Weeks passed without a response from Barron, and Decatur may have hoped the matter was closed. But then at the end of November, Barron sent him a very long letter of about five thousand words that expressed an intensity and self-righteousness that was altogether new. It was couched in terms of a manifesto, as if Barron were addressing posterity and wanted all his injuries and self-justifications entered into the historical record.

Once again, the letter is designed to provoke. The insulting quality of the jibes—"your contumacious . . . remarks," "your malicious design," "your machinations against me"—is more pointed than in previous correspondence.

It is a sad and muddled document, filled with bluster and self-pity. Only in the closing paragraphs does Barron return to the possibility of a duel, and then he again clings to his contorted logic that somehow it is Decatur who has done the challenging:

> *SIR: . . . It is true, you have never given me a direct, formal, and written, invitation to meet you in the field, such as one gentleman of honor <u>ought</u> to send to another. But, if your own admissions, that you had "incautiously said you would meet me if I wished it," . . . do not amount to a challenge, I cannot comprehend the object or import of such declarations . . . I consider you as having thrown down the gauntlet, and I have no hesitation in accepting it. . . . All I demand is to be placed upon equal grounds with you; such as two honorable men may decide upon, <u>as just and proper.</u>*

Barron, having spent over four thousand words trying to bring about a duel, then felt constrained to include his own condemnation of the practice:

> *Upon the subject of dueling, I perfectly coincide with the opinions you have expressed. I consider it as a barborous practice which ought to be exploded from civilized society; but, sir, there may be causes of such extra-ordinary and aggravated insult and injury, received by an individual, as to render an appeal to arms, on his part, absolutely necessary; mine I con-*

ceive to be a case of that description. . . . And now, sir, I have only to add, that, if you will make known your determination, and the name of your friend, I will give that of mine, in order to complete the necessary arrangements to a final close of this affair.

I am, sir, your obedient servant,

JAMES BARRON

For all his posturing, Barron was clearly moving closer to a challenge, and it was becoming more and more likely that a duel could not be avoided. When the challenge came, Decatur knew he would have to respond. And in order to do so, he would need to find a second.

One of the visitors to Washington that December was Commodore Charles Morris, who was on his way to Venezuela to resume the diplomatic negotiations with Bolívar that Perry had opened. Morris and Decatur were particularly close. Their friendship went back to 1804 when Morris, then a midshipman, played an instrumental role in the capture and burning of the *Philadelphia*.

At his Navy Board office, Decatur showed Morris the last lengthy letter from Barron. He told Morris he did not want to fight, but felt constrained to do so should Barron demand it, and asked Morris to serve as his second, or "friend." Morris declined, pointing out that his sailing orders precluded such a commitment. He pointed out to Decatur that Barron had no reason to challenge, since Decatur had given him no cause. He urged Decatur to send Barron a clear, straightforward account of what he had in fact said. Such a letter would force Barron to back down, since it would make it evident that Decatur, while strongly opposed to Barron's return to active duty, had in no way impugned his honor.

Decatur declined to do so, Morris wrote, "because it might have the *appearance* to some of too earnest a wish on his part to avoid meeting Commodore Barron." Morris protested. He argued that Decatur's courage was established beyond all question, and "that so far as being injurious to his reputation, such a statement of facts would elevate it still higher and that the improvement of so favorable an opportunity for setting a good example to the younger officers of the navy was required from him by the highest considerations."

With Decatur's reluctant assistance, Morris then drew up a draft of a short letter that explained all. Decatur went over it carefully, and admitted it to be correct on every count, but refused to sign it. A frustrated Morris wrote, "He appeared to be governed by an apprehension that his reputation might suffer if he took any means to avoid a meeting with Commodore Barron, if Barron had any disposition to bring about one."

Both Decatur and Barron were anxious that their wives not learn of their quarrel, and each made every effort to keep the news of it private. But the two men were simply too prominent in their professional sphere for their dispute to remain entirely secret—Barron was third in seniority on the navy list, and Decatur was fifth—and inevitably, word of their feud became common gossip in the higher naval circles.

Still looking for a second after being turned down by Commodore Morris, Decatur approached both of his fellow commissioners, Rodgers and Porter. They too refused him, citing much the same arguments used by Morris—that there was insufficient cause for a duel, and that Decatur's courage had been proved beyond question.

The refusal of so many high-ranking officers to serve as Decatur's second raised an interesting possibility. The *code duello* stipulated that the seconds of duelists must be of similar rank and standing to the men they represented. If Decatur was not able to find such a second, the duel—if it ever came to that—might have to be canceled by default. While this intriguing irony was still making the rounds in late December, something quite extraordinary occurred in Washington, an event of such passing strangeness as to be deemed inexplicable unless seen in terms of a deliberate conspiracy.

One afternoon just before Christmas, as Decatur was about to cross the avenue on his way home from his office, he was surprised when a carriage suddenly stopped in front of him and Commodore William Bainbridge, wreathed in smiles and radiating good cheer, emerged and greeted him warmly. Bainbridge had deliberately avoided Decatur and had not spoken to him since their bitter falling out in the Mediterranean in 1815.

"Decatur, I have behaved like a great fool," he now gushed, "but I hope you will forgive me. You have always contrived to reap laurels from my misfortunes."

What had provoked the effusive professions of friendship after all the years of silence? A startled and perhaps puzzled Decatur invited Bainbridge home for a glass of wine. He declined, citing a prior appointment, but promised to return to Washington in a few days, and then invited himself as a guest at the Decaturs' home.

That evening, when Decatur told Susan of his unexpected little adventure, she was immediately suspicious. "I said to my husband that it seemed to me an act of great assurance to invite himself to be our guest after allowing five years to elapse without speaking or writing to him when there had been no cause of offense, especially as he had been several weeks in Washington; and I was afraid he had some other motive than that of true repentance!"

Decatur was not naive. He almost certainly discerned the real reason behind Bainbridge's sudden change of heart. It would have been obvious enough that Bainbridge was deliberately placing himself in a position to serve as Decatur's "friend" should there be a challenge.

As promised, Bainbridge returned just after Christmas and moved in with the Decaturs. Susan, who knew nothing of her husband's protracted correspondence with Barron, nor of its likely outcome, continued to be suspicious. Decatur simply accepted the situation.

Decatur still owed Barron an answer to his long, rambling letter of the previous month, and at the end of the year he finally got around to writing it. It expressed a new impatience, a put-up-or-shut-up irritation he had not previously employed.

Sir: . . . It was my determination, on the receipt of your letter, not to notice it; but, upon more mature reflection, I conceive, that as I have suffered myself to be drawn into this unprofitable discussion, I ought not to leave the false coloring and calumnies, which you have introduced into your letter, unanswered. . . . Instead of calling me out for injuries which you chose to insist that I have heaped upon you, you have thought fit to enter into this war of words. I reiterate to you, that I have not challenged, nor do I intend to challenge you. . . . If we fight, it must be of your seeking; and you must take all the risk and all the inconvenience which usually attend the challenger, in such cases.

His blunt closing made his sentiments unambiguous:

I have now to inform you, that I shall pay no further attention to any communication you may make to me, other than a direct call to the field.

Your obed't servant,
STEPHEN DECATUR

Decatur's letter forced Barron at last to abandon his insistence that Decatur had somehow already issued a challenge. If the two were to fight, it must be by Barron's choice. Reluctantly, Barron finally threw down the gauntlet. When his challenge finally came, it was curiously equivocal.

Sir: Your letter of the 29th ult. I have received. In it you say that you have now to inform me that you shall pay no further attention to any communication that I may make to you other than a direct call to the field; in answer to which I have only to reply, that whenever you will consent to meet me on fair and equal grounds, that is, such as two honorable men may consider just and proper, you are at liberty to view this as that call. . . .

I am, sir, yours, &c.
JAMES BARRON

No matter how clumsily presented, Barron had at last brought the issue to a head, and by a coincidence that was hardly accidental, the challenge arrived at a time when William Bainbridge was in residence at Decatur House. Decatur showed him Barron's letter and formally asked him to serve as his friend. As expected, Bainbridge accepted on the spot, and Decatur was able to reply to Barron by the next mail:

> *Sir: I have received your communication of the 16th and am at a loss to know what your intention is. If you intended it as a challenge, I accept it, and refer you to my friend Com. Bainbridge, who is fully authorized by me to make any arrangement he chooses, as regards weapons, mode, or distance.*
>
> *Your obedient servant,*
> STEPHEN DECATUR

As the challenged party, Decatur had the right to specify almost all the details of the duel, such as the date, place, the choice of weapons, the distance between the duelists, and the specific rules that would govern the fight. But the only detail he cared about was the location. He wanted the fight to be close to home in case he was seriously wounded. On February 10, 1820, he sent his instructions to Bainbridge, who had moved on board the USS *Columbus*, moored below Washington at St. Mary's, Maryland.

> *Dear Bainbridge, I have received yours of the 6th. I regret that this tedious and troublesome business of mine should deprive you of the pleasure of visiting your friends. The place we are to meet is entirely at our option. Their convenience will not be consulted. My preference to some point near this arises from the convenience of a man's lying wounded at a distance from his own house; and as both of us cannot be indulged in being near our homes, I should not like to yield to them this point, unless you should find it inconvenient to come thus far. I leave you entirely the choice of weapons and distance, as also the time. I beg, however, unless it*

will inconvenience you very much, that Bladensburg, near the city of
Washington, may be the point of meeting.

Yours sincerely,
STEPHEN DECATUR

To no one's surprise Barron selected Jesse Elliott to serve as his friend,
but it was not for another fortnight that Bainbridge finally met from him
on board the *Columbus* to complete the arrangements. As soon as their
meeting was over Bainbridge sent Decatur a copy of the terms that would
govern the duel:

March 8, 1820

It is agreed by the undersigned, as friends of Commodore Decatur and
Commodore Barron, that the meeting, which is to take place at nine
A.M., on the 22nd instant, shall take place at Bladensburg, near the
district of Columbia, and that the weapons shall be pistols; the distance
eight paces or yards; that, previously to firing, the parties shall be
directed to present, and shall not fire before the word "one" is given, or
after the word "three"; that the words, <u>one, two, three,</u> shall be given
by Commodore Bainbridge.

The shocking arrangements formalized by Bainbridge and Elliott were
far from ordinary terms for a duel, and made it almost certain that at least
one of the participants would die. The usual distance for pistol duels was
ten or twelve paces, that is, thirty or thirty-six feet. Elliott had pleaded that
Barron was shortsighted, and that bringing the two men closer to eight
paces, or twenty-four feet, would help his principal. But how could it help
Decatur? It only made a fatal shot more likely. But there was another condition that vastly increased the danger, particularly for Decatur. Under the
generally accepted conditions for dueling, the two antagonists stood facing
each other across the agreed distance, either with their pistols at their sides,
or with their arms cocked and their pistols at head level. At the signal, each

man had to quickly bring his pistol forward and aim before firing. In the hurry to get off a shot, misses were frequent. But the Bainbridge–Elliott conditions called for the duelists to present—that is, aim—before the signal to fire, so that each was drawing a bead on the other and at the word had only to pull the trigger.

Decatur had already confided to friends that he had no desire to injure Barron, or to lose his own life, and that he intended to fire wide, either into the air or into the ground. He thought it probable that if he could indicate his intention to Barron by deliberately failing to aim, Barron was likely to do the same. But with both men forced to aim their pistols before the signal, there was no way either could indicate to the other an intention to fire wide.

Years later, Susan Decatur wrote: "When he received the letter of Commodore Bainbridge detailing the desperate terms that he had arranged for the meeting with Commodore Barron, my husband showed it to his colleagues, Commodore Rodgers and Commodore Porter, and stated that when he accepted the challenge it was his intention not to fire his pistol, but the terms imposed were so desperate that he would wound him in the hip. Both the gentlemen told him that by pursuing that course he would greatly increase his own danger. He replied that he could not help it; that he would rather lose his own life ten or fifteen years sooner than to take the life of any individual against whom he had no ill will!"

The most important social event of the Washington season that year was the marriage of the president's daughter, Maria Monroe, to Samuel J. Gouvernor. A round of parties had been arranged to celebrate the occasion, the first of which was a ball given by the Decaturs. The date was Saturday, March 18, just four days before the scheduled duel. One of the guests that evening has left us his impressions of the host: "He seemed out of spirits, and I was particularly struck by the solemnity of his manner and his devotion to his wife and her music, as she played upon the harp, the company forming a semicircle in front of her, Decatur himself in uniform the centre of the semicircle, his eyes riveted upon his wife."

Another guest, Commodore David Porter, had already sent out invitations for a similar party in honor of the bridal couple to be held a few days hence. At a private moment during the festivities, Decatur drew him aside and told him, "I may spoil your party."

NINETEEN

Bladensburg

Soon after daybreak on the morning of March 22, Stephen Decatur quietly let himself out of his home on President's Square. Turning toward Pennsylvania Avenue, he made his way on foot through the still empty streets to Beale's Hotel, on Capitol Hill, where by prearrangement he met with his second, William Bainbridge, and Samuel Hambleton, the purser on the USS *Columbus* and an old friend. The two men had come up to Washington the day before from St. Mary's, where their ship was fitting out, and had spent the night at the hotel. Hambleton had already ordered breakfast for the three, and while they ate, they went over plans for the morning.

Decatur seemed in good spirits. He and Susan had stayed late the previous night at a cotillion hosted by their neighbors, John Quincy and Louisa Adams, and despite his lack of sleep he seemed cheerful and rested. He had worn his dress uniform at the party, resplendent with gold braid and glittering decorations, but this morning he was in deliberately subdued mufti, a precaution against attracting unwanted attention.

The men discussed the coming duel, and Hambleton made note of the fact that Decatur evinced no animosity toward Barron and specifically stated that he did not wish to kill him. He had brought a new will with him, which he needed to sign in the presence of three witnesses. It left everything to Susan. Since he did not want to advertise his presence by finding a third witness in the hotel, he told the others he would put off signing it until later.

After breakfast, the three climbed into a hired carriage for the short journey to Bladensburg on the Baltimore–Washington stage road. Shortly after leaving the District of Columbia and crossing into Maryland they spotted Jesse Elliott standing beside the road on the brow of a hill, waiting for them. Bainbridge and Hambleton got out and spoke briefly with him before making their way on foot to the dueling grounds. Decatur, walking alone, followed at a distance. The place was a large open area, not far from the eastern branch of the Potomac, and screened from the road by trees and shrubbery. In the two decades since the founding of Washington, some fifty duels had already been fought there, earning it the name of the Valley of Chance.

Commodore Barron, along with a Dr. Hall, and Barron's young nephew Edward Latimer, soon arrived on the field. They had come up by steamer from Hampton Roads the previous day and had spent the night in Bladensburg. The two principals, standing about forty feet apart, bowed formally to each other. The seconds, Bainbridge and Elliott, went to the center of the field to confer. The supernumeraries, Hambleton and Latimer, stood near their principals. They were there to fetch carriages, relay messages, and act as stage managers. Their basic function, to help move the wounded and dead, was rarely alluded to.

It was a cold, overcast morning, and all wore overcoats—the narrow-waisted, flared surcoats then in fashion—against the chill winds coming off the unseen river. Spring was just beginning to manifest itself. The landscape was still defined by wintery browns and grays, and at that early hour the men's breath hung in the air as they spoke. While Decatur and Barron talked quietly with their supernumeraries, the seconds went over the final details and marked off the eight-yard distance that would separate the two combatants. Dr. Hall, the surgeon whom Barron had brought with him from Virginia, stood to the side alone, his satchel close at hand, ready to perform whatever grim work might lie ahead.

Decatur knew that his own surgeons were present, but hidden from sight somewhere in the surrounding woods. While dueling was generally tolerated, his doctors preferred to distance themselves from such potentially scandalous activities if at all possible. They assured Decatur that they would be ready if he needed them, but should their services not be required, they could discreetly return to Washington after the encounter, their presence at the scene unnoticed and unremarked.

Bainbridge was normally a deliberative, phlegmatic man, but he had been notably agitated at breakfast, and his nervousness had only increased during the ride out of the city. One of his assigned tasks was to load the pistols, and Decatur could not help but notice that he was having inordinate difficulty, and offered to take over. Because it was not strictly within the rules, he asked Elliott if he had any objection. When he received a confused shrug in answer, he gently took the pistols out of Bainbridge's hands, emptied them, and began loading them again. Moments later, Decatur, who had little appreciation of irony, carefully seated and rammed home the ball that would soon kill him.

The pistols were elegant artifacts, exquisitely engraved specimens of the gunsmith's art. But even the most carefully crafted handguns were subject to all sorts of problems. Decatur was well aware that a dampness of powder, or a fouled touchhole, could cause a pistol to hang fire, and if the flint was poorly adjusted, the weapon might not fire at all. If there was insufficient gunpowder in the chamber, the ball would have too little velocity. But to overload the pistol might cause it to explode, killing or injuring the man who pulled the trigger rather than his opponent.

Decatur looked over at the man whose challenge had brought him to the field. Barron was standing with his teenaged nephew Edward Latimer, who was clearly too young to handle the grim duties on a field of honor. He was obviously deeply attached to his uncle and was trying not to weep. Barron was kept busy comforting him.

It was literally the first time Decatur had laid eyes on Barron since the *Chesapeake* court-martial twelve years earlier. The only contact between the two men since that time had been through the correspondence that had led to his challenge. Barron was somewhat whiter and slower than Decatur remembered, but still very much the same man he had been in the old days, tall, robust, and with a round, amiable face and thoughtful manner, the same man that Decatur had once loved as his own father.

But that morning Decatur's mind was almost certainly focused not on the past but on the perilous work at hand, and specifically on the properties of the pistol with which he would soon defend his honor. Dueling pistols were by design notoriously inaccurate. The dueling code forbade the use of rifled barrels, which improved accuracy, and while Decatur knew how to compensate for the "dispart," or throw, of a pistol, each weapon was handmade, and differed somewhat from all others. There was no way to predict with any precision where the ball might go unless one had fired the same pistol a number of times.

For some reason the proceedings seemed to take an inordinate amount of time. It was not until forty-five minutes after their arrival on the field that all was finally ready. The two seconds tossed for position, and Bainbridge won. Decatur opted to stand to the north, at a point that was slightly lower than the southern position. It made little difference. Neither duelist would have the sun in his eyes on such an overcast day.

The two men stepped to their marks and faced each other. Bainbridge went over the details one last time. He explained that he would first give the order to present, that is, to cock their weapons and take aim, then he would count out the numbers "one-two-three." The duelists were instructed not to fire before hearing the word "one," or after hearing the word "three."

It was well known that Bainbridge, particularly when nervous, had a habit of prefacing any statement with an involuntary sound like "un-ter," or "un-to," as if clearing his throat before actually speaking. It occurred to Barron that this idiosyncrasy might come out sounding like "one-two," and he asked Bainbridge to demonstrate precisely how he planned to give the order. Bainbridge obliged, repeating the entire order, "present . . . one-two-three," and Barron, satisfied, thanked him.

As the seconds moved to their position, there was a last moment of silence. The two men tensed. Bainbridge opened his mouth to give the order, when, unexpectedly, Decatur raised his hand, and said, "Oh, there is one thing I insist on. I insist on a search."

Captain Elliott, his body tensed in anticipation of the drama of the moment, was clearly upset by this unexpected interruption. "Commodore Decatur, what do you mean?" he asked sharply.

"I do not wish to be shielded," Decatur explained. "See here!" With his left hand, he pulled some flints out of his vest pocket, which, innocent in themselves, could conceivably have been solid enough to deflect a shot.

Decatur was not about to be put off by the anger of someone like Elliott. "I insist on being searched," he said calmly, in a tone that would not brook denial. Elliott bristled. "Elliott, Elliott," Barron said mildly, "remember what you've been told, and do your duty." Then, holding open his arms to show that he hid nothing, he said, "I'm willing to be searched. I certainly wish for no unfair advantage." Bainbridge stepped forward to check Barron's pockets, while an angry Elliott made a hurried show of examining Decatur. By now Elliott was as nervous as Bainbridge. Had that been Decatur's motive for demanding a search? Or had he hoped that by breaking the rhythm of the ritual, he might encourage Barron to have a last-minute change of heart?

After the interruption all parties returned to their previous positions. Bainbridge prepared once again to give the order to present, when Barron unexpectedly said, "I hope, Commodore Decatur, that when we meet in another world, we shall be better friends than we have been in this."

Decatur answered flatly, "I have never been your enemy, sir."

It was an extraordinary moment, and strictly against the rules. According to the traditions of the code, once a challenge had been made and accepted, the two duelists were not allowed to communicate, except through their seconds. Barron and Decatur had not only spoken directly to each other, they had made statements that appeared to resolve their differences. It was the duty of the seconds to attempt to bring about a reconciliation between the two quarreling parties. Elliott and Bainbridge should have immediately suspended the proceedings and questioned both men to ascertain whether the statements just made had canceled the reason for the duel. But it was clear that neither of the seconds had the slightest intention of halting the proceedings.

Elliott said sternly, "Gentlemen, your places," and Bainbridge followed up immediately with the order, "Present!"

The principals raised their pistols. Each aimed at the exact same spot: his opponent's hip.

Bainbridge said clearly, "One. Two . . ."

Both weapons fired simultaneously. It was said later that the balls must have passed within an inch of each other. Barron was hit and pulled around by the force of the ball. He fell instantly, saying, "You must excuse my quitting the ground. I can stand no longer." It was evident that Decatur had been hit as well, but he remained on his feet, momentarily dazed. Then, as the color drained from his face, he dropped his pistol and put his hand to the wound, saying quietly, "Oh, lord, I am a dead man." Then he too, dropped.

Bainbridge and Hambleton ran over and tried to prop him up, but it was evident that he could not stand, and they gently lowered him again to the ground. The two duelists were now lying within fifteen feet of each other, each convinced he was mortally wounded. Barron called out, "Gentlemen, everything has been conducted in a most honorable manner. Decatur, I forgive you from the bottom of my heart." Decatur, speaking weakly, responded in kind. The two, each in great pain, exchanged a few words. One of those present described the scene as the end of a great tragedy: Hamlet and Laertes.

Suddenly, there were people everywhere. Friends and allies of Decatur who had been hiding in the woods poured out onto the field. The once empty dueling grounds now teemed with life. Two doctors—Baily Washington and a Dr. Trevitt—hurried to Decatur's side, followed by both of his fellow commissioners, John Rodgers and David Porter, and a number of other officials. As the spectators made their way to the fallen commodores there was a shout, and everyone on the field looked up to see an astonishing and scandalous sight. Jesse Elliott had panicked when he saw both men fall, and fearing that he might be charged for his role in their deaths, had commandeered Barron's carriage and run off, fleeing helter-skelter toward the state line, deserting Barron and the rest of his party. An enraged David Porter threw himself on his horse and raced after him, catching up about a mile from the field, where the driver had stopped to repair a broken trace. Elliott, more frightened than embarrassed, jumped out of the carriage and called out to Porter, "How do things fare on the ground?"

"They fare so badly, sir," Porter snapped back angrily, "that you left your friend weltering in his blood upon the bare earth. Go back and do what you can to lessen the mischief you have aided in committing; go back and do your duty to your wounded friend!" Then he wheeled and returned to the field.

By this time Dr. Hall had examined Barron's wound and diagnosed it as serious but not fatal. The two doctors attending Decatur probed his wound and quickly discovered that the ball had severed vital arteries. He might live for a time—perhaps several hours—but there was no way to stem the flow, and the wound meant certain death. Decatur took the news stoically, saying only that he would have preferred to die on the quarter-deck.

Rodgers stepped toward Barron and stood over him scowling, but saying nothing. Barron, equally silent, returned the stare. There was no love lost between the two. They had not seen each other since Rodgers had deliberately snubbed Barron in Washington on his return to America. After a while, Rodgers, still scowling, turned away and went off to check on Decatur. A little later he returned, and looking down on Barron, asked, "Are you much hurt?"

Barron's reply is worth quoting in full. "Sir, when I last did you the honor to salute you, you did not return the compliment; and until that conduct is atoned for you need never expect to receive an answer from me to any question you may feel disposed to ask." This statement, from a man lying wounded, who had just been informed that his bullet had mortally wounded the nation's greatest hero while he himself would survive, is perhaps the clearest indication we have of Barron's almost pathetic sense of injured pride.

Rodgers, infuriated, was about to respond angrily, when Porter, who had returned, intervened. "Commodore Rodgers! This is neither the time nor the place for further altercation," he said firmly, and led him away.

Samuel Hambleton had by this time climbed up to the road and returned with the hired carriage, and he and Bainbridge and Rodgers managed to lift Decatur into it for the return to Washington. Decatur's head rested on Rodgers's shoulder. Dr. Trevitt climbed in to minister to the stricken man. Decatur suggested weakly that they take Barron with them, but there was no room. As the carriage left, Barron called out, "God bless you, Decatur," and heard the faint reply, "Farewell, farewell, Barron."

Bainbridge did not accompany Decatur. Undoubtedly harboring the same fears that had caused Elliott to bolt, he hurried off in another carriage, bound for the Washington Navy Yard, where a tender was waiting to take him down the Potomac and out of the District of Columbia. Porter stayed behind and waited for Elliott to return with the carriage. When he failed to appear, Porter eventually went up to the road, halted a passing carriage, and ordered it down to where Barron lay. He and Latimer gently lifted Barron into it, and with Dr. Hall in attendance and Porter trotting alongside on his horse, they started for the city.

They came upon Elliott just across the state line. He was moving very slowly back to the dueling field, obviously hoping to delay his return until everyone had left. All innocence, Elliott poked his head out of the window and asked Porter, "How do matters stand?" Porter jumped off his horse and pulled Elliott bodily from his carriage, forcing him into the carriage with Barron. "Your place is here, sir, alongside your wounded friend," he said angrily, "I insist upon your getting in."

Elliott was nothing if not brazen. He immediately tried to distance himself from the tragedy, and to lay the blame on others. Leaning out the window, he said to Porter, "It's too bad that Bainbridge could not consent to an accommodation before the firing." Porter, outraged by Elliott's hypocrisy, refused to reply, and leaving the carriage to proceed as best it could, galloped off to Washington. Never, for the rest of his life, did he ever speak to Elliott again.

Soon after, the carriage carrying the dying Decatur reached his home on President's Square. Commodore Rodgers, his clothing caked with the blood of the fallen hero, got out and knocked on the door. Susan Decatur was still at breakfast with her nieces, who were house guests. She hurried to the door to receive what would be the cruelest and most terrible shock of her life.

TWENTY

Afterwards

Stephen Decatur's death generated less attention in the nation's news-papers and opinion journals than might have been expected for such an admired and colorful celebrity. The obituaries were laudatory but generally subdued. The reason, of course, was the manner of his dying. Even adherents of dueling admitted it was a distasteful practice at best, and the fulsome encomiums and worshipful lamentations that might otherwise have been his were muted by embarrassed references to the Bladensburg meeting.

In an attempt to make it clear that Decatur had not sought the confrontation, a group of his friends arranged to publish the full text of the correspondence that had led to the challenge between the two commodores. It was hastily printed in pamphlet form and quickly copied by newspapers across the country. The letters showed clearly that the quarrel had originated with Barron, that Decatur had never sought a duel, that he disapproved of the practice, and that he had only reluctantly accepted a call to the field. But to the surprise of some of Decatur's supporters, not every reader chose to interpret the evidence in a light favorable to Decatur. There were complaints about his lack of civility, and one Delaware newspaper charged that his "stinging sarcasm, sneering hauteur, and vindictive accusation . . . were enough to drive any man in Barron's circumstances to desperation."

For months after the duel Susan was inconsolable, and it is fair to say that never, in the remaining forty years of her life, did she ever recover from the shock. When she was told that a sailor had said that Decatur's death meant that the navy had lost its mainmast, her response was, "With me it is far worse; it is total, total wreck!" Decatur had left her his entire estate, worth more than seventy-five thousand dollars, enough for her to live out her life in comfort, even luxury, but through her own heedless extravagance and the mismanagement of the funds by trusted friends, she quickly frittered away the entire fortune.

She was forced to sell Decatur House, which was promptly transformed into the French legation. She moved into Kalorama, which she rented to be near her departed husband. When she could no longer afford the rent, she moved again, this time to Georgetown, and became a virtual recluse. She had no illusions concerning the genesis of the tragedy. She never blamed Barron, but saved her fury and distrust for Elliott and Bainbridge. At one point she wrote to Henry Clay that she no longer dared to attend any public events because she might "encounter my husband's murderers!"

In 1826, prodded by Susan and influential friends of her late husband, Congress once again took up the matter of prize money for the capture and destruction of the *Philadelphia*. The bill passed easily in the Senate, but ran into obstructions in the House, where opponents objected to methods of payment. In time, the bill died in committee. Another attempt was made in 1834, with the same result. In 1837 she received a pension of fifty dollars a month from the government, but this was canceled in 1842. In 1849 Susan presented a final memorial to Congress supporting her claim for prize money for the *Philadelphia,* and this too failed. To this day, Congress has never seen fit to honor the Decatur claim.

Susan died in 1860 in the Georgetown Visitation Convent, having converted to the Catholic Church some time around 1828. She was the last, and in many ways the most tragic, victim of Stephen Decatur's stubborn effort to protect the honor of the navy.

For years following the duel James Barron remained under a cloud. His reputation, already in eclipse as a result of his 1808 court-martial, gained fresh notoriety after he killed Decatur, but far more damaging to his career were the charges hanging over him that predated the duel. He was able to disprove the rumor that he had sailed under British license during the war, but the other two charges, that he had made disloyal and possibly treasonous statements to the British consul in Pernambuco in 1809, and that he had not made sufficient effort to return home to defend his country after war was declared in 1812, continued to haunt him.

In 1821, at Barron's request, the navy convened a court of inquiry to examine both charges. The court eventually found that the treasonous comments that Barron had allegedly made to the British consul in Pernambuco had "not been proven." On the second charge, "the court is further of opinion, that, although the evidence produced by Captain Barron establishes his sincere and earnest desire to return to the United States at certain periods, and the difficulty of accomplishing his wishes, yet the court is of the opinion, that the evidence of his inability to return sooner than he actually did, is not satisfactory; and it is, therefore, the opinion of the court, that his absence from the United States, without the permission of the government, was contrary to his duty as an officer in the navy of the United States." Barron, by the court's finding, had demonstrated a lack of zeal, a failing to which no punishment was attached.

After her husband's death, Susan Decatur is said to have extracted a promise from President Monroe never to offer Barron a sea command, a promise that he and his successors honored. But the Virginia caucus continued to press Barron's case, and Monroe, toward the end of his administration, did in fact appoint him commandant of the Philadelphia Navy Yard. Once returned to active service, Barron continued to perform various shore duties until 1838, when he was virtually retired. By the time he died in 1852, he was the senior officer in the navy.

Only a few weeks after the duel, Commodore William Bainbridge set sail in the USS *Columbus* to take command of the Mediterranean squadron. It was to be his last sea duty. The controversy surrounding his role in the duel had long since died down by the time he returned from the Mediterranean and had little effect on his subsequent career. One of his later assignments was to succeed John Rodgers as the president of the Board of Navy Commissioners.

Bainbridge, like Barron, suffered from delicate health, which in his case was exacerbated by poor medical care. Toward the end of his life he became addicted to drugs originally prescribed as painkillers and cough suppressants, and as a result in his last years he became subject to sudden mood shifts and extended bouts of depression. He died in 1833. At his specific request, his daughters burned almost all of his personal papers. Although Bainbridge never gave a reason for ordering his papers destroyed, his biographer, David F. Long, was convinced it was to hide his complicity in bringing on the Barron-Decatur duel.

Jesse Duncan Elliott remained a troublemaker and scapegrace to the end. In his later years his career prospects were improved considerably by his friendship with President Andrew Jackson, a maverick in his own right who was drawn to Elliott's contrarian personality and unconventional character. But even friends in high places could not save Elliott from his own excesses. In 1840, after his return from a stormy tour of duty as commander of the Mediterranean squadron, he was court-martialed at the request of his subordinates. He was found guilty of a number of charges and suspended from the service for four years. His sentence was later commuted, and he returned to active duty. He died in 1845.

Stephen Decatur remained almost as popular in death as he had been in life. But the navy itself, once the darling of the public for its many celebrated feats of valor in the War of 1812, lost a great deal of its prestige in the aftermath of the duel. The fact that so many high-ranking officers had known of the quarrel beforehand and had done so little to quash it, and the fact that Barron, Elliott, and Bainbridge continued to hold positions of high honor despite their involvement in Decatur's death, did not sit well with most Americans.

Commodore John Rodgers, always an astute politician, understood the importance of popular support and recognized that the public's change of heart relative to the navy did not bode well for the service. He also recognized that Decatur's popularity could translate into extra votes for the navy in Congress, and he made it a matter of Navy Board policy to keep the memory of his friend before the public.

The most prominent symbol of Decatur was the USS *Macedonian*, the trophy ship he had captured from the British in 1812, and Rodgers saw to it that she remained on active duty and was kept in the public eye as much as possible. By the 1830s, when it became clear that the *Macedonian* was no longer seaworthy, and was in fact beyond repair, Rodgers refused to order her broken up. He arranged for a new *Macedonian* to be built to plans based on the British original, and then claimed she was the same ship, rebuilt.

But by that time a resurrected *Macedonian* was no longer deemed sufficient to keep Decatur's memory fresh before the public, and in 1838 a sloop of war, the USS *Decatur*, was launched, providing a more traditional memorial. She became the first of a line of five USS *Decatur*s commissioned over the years, the most recent of which is the Aegis Class destroyer DDG-73, commissioned in 1998.

In 1846, as the once-grand estate of Kalorama fell into disrepair, a committee was formed in Philadelphia to bring Decatur's remains home to the city in which he grew up. With the sanction of the bereaved Susan, Decatur's casket was removed from Washington and returned to Philadelphia, and with solemn ceremony reinterred near the tomb of his parents in St. Peter's churchyard.

In the commemorative speeches given on the occasion, the local dignitaries, proud to have Philadelphia's greatest warrior restored to his native city, made repeated references to his childhood, his many deeds of valor, his famous toast with its provocative "right or wrong" declaration, and predictably, the family motto that he and his father had so conspicuously lived by: *Pro libertate et patria dulce periculum*.

Almost certainly unremarked on that occasion would have been the singular phrase that a triumphant Decatur had so casually coined on the spur of the moment in 1815, when a threatening Algerian admiral had demanded: *"Dove andante?"*

"Dove mi piace!" he had shouted back.

It was quintessential Decatur. *I go where I please!* Direct. Unambiguous. And with a touch of swagger. A fitting battle cry for the man, for his navy, and for the boisterous, restless country he served so well and did so much to define.

Acknowledgments

For many years my friend the naval scholar W. M. P. Dunne planned a biography of Stephen Decatur. But Bill Dunne died in 1995, and the book he had so long researched died with him. I am sure my version of Decatur's life differs significantly from the one Bill might have written—we often had friendly arguments over our interpretations of the story—but every biographer sees his subject in a uniquely personal light. Bill was a prodigious researcher and left copious notes on Decatur's life. Perhaps some fortunate writer in the future will access them to write the book that Bill planned.

Writing is a famously solitary act, but it almost always requires the help of others. I am particularly grateful for the support I have received once again from Paul O'Pecko and his staff at the G. W. Blunt White Library at the Mystic Seaport Museum, as well as the staffs of the Stonington (Connecticut) Free Library and the Westerly (Rhode Island) Public Library. I need to thank several naval scholars for their generous help, most particularly Frederick C. Leiner, who saved me from making several egregious errors, as well as Tyrone Martin, and William Dudley. I owe a very special thanks to Stephen Decatur, Jr., and his wife, Marcia, of Marblehead, Massachusetts, for sharing with me some priceless pieces of family memorabilia relating to "the Commodore." I want to thank my agent, Al Zuckerman, whose sound judgment and good taste always provide the right leavening of objectivity to what is at heart a subjective endeavor; my editor Bill Rosen, an editor who really edits, and whose formidable erudition and uncanny skill in untangling some of my less judicious rhetoric has been key; and the most important member of my support team, my wife, Belinda, who remains, quite literally, my inspiration.

Bibliography

While this book was written for a general audience rather than for specialists, naval scholars may want to know something of my sources. There were five specific interpretive works that were so central to my understanding of Stephen Decatur and his times that I feel obliged to single them out for special attribution. These include what seem to me the two most authoritative biographies of Decatur, those of Alexander Slidell Mackenzie (1848) and Charles Lee Lewis (1937), as well as two very different histories of the early navy, *The Commodores,* by Leonard F. Guttridge and J. D. Smith, and *A Gentlemanly and Honorable Profession* by Christopher McKee, and lastly, a long article by W. M. P. Dunne, "Pistols and Honor: The James Barron–Stephen Decatur Conflict, 1798–1807," in *The American Neptune* (Volume L, 1990). Each of these works was, in its own way, crucial to my understanding of a complicated story, and they inform every page of my book. In addition, I was fortunate, thanks particularly to the generosity of Stephen Decatur, Jr., of Marblehead, Massachusetts, to be able to call upon a wide variety of primary material, including Secretary Crowninshield's unusual private letter of March 14, 1815 to Stephen Decatur, and Susan Decatur's remarkable *Memorial,* which I had been led to believe had been lost forever.

A more complete listing of works I have consulted and found helpful includes:

Adair, Douglass. *Fame and the Founding Fathers.* New York: W.W. Norton, 1974.

Anthony, Irvin. *Decatur.* New York: Scribner's, 1931.

Baldick, Robert. *The Duel: A History* (reprint). New York: Barnes and Noble, 1996.

Beach, Edward L. *The United States Navy: 200 Years.* New York: Henry Holt & Company, 1986.

Beale, Marie. *Decatur House and Its Inhabitants.* Washington: National Trust for Historic Preservation, 1954.

Bradford, James C., ed. *Command Under Sail: Makers of the American Naval Tradition 1775–1850.* Annapolis: Naval Institute Press, 1985.

Brady, Cyrus Townsend. *Stephen Decatur.* Boston: Small, Maynard & Co., 1900.

Cooper, James Fenimore. *History of the Navy of the United States of America,* introduction by Edward L. Beach. Annapolis: Naval Institute Press, 2001.

Decatur, Susan. *Memorial to the President and Members of the Senate.* November 24, 1849.

de Kay, James Tertius. *The Battle of Stonington: Torpedoes, Submarines and Rockets in the War of 1812.* Annapolis: Naval Institute Press, 1990.

————. *Chronicles of the Frigate Macedonian 1809–1922.* New York: W.W. Norton, 1995.

Dudley, William S., ed. *The Naval War of 1812: A Documentary History,* vols. I and II. Washington: Naval Historical Center, 1985 and 1992.

Dye, Ira. *The Fatal Cruise of the Argus: Two Captains in the War of 1812.* Annapolis: Naval Institute Press, 1994.

Fleming, Thomas. *Duel: Alexander Hamilton, Aaron Burr and the Future of America.* New York: Basic Books, 1999.

Forester, C. S. *The Age of Fighting Sail: The Story of The Naval War of 1812.* Garden City, N.Y.: Doubleday & Company, 1956.

Freeman, Joanne B. *Affairs of Honor: National Politics in the New Republic.* New Haven: Yale University Press, 2001.

Gardiner, Robert, ed. *The Naval War of 1812.* London: Chatham Publishing, 1998.

Guttridge, Leonard F., and Smith, J. D. *The Commodores.* Annapolis: Naval Institute Press (reprint), no date.

Hubbard, H. *Congressional Speech in favor of compensation for Susan Decatur.* April 19, 1834.

Hutcheon, Wallace, Jr. *Robert Fulton: Pioneer of Undersea Warfare.* Annapolis: Naval Institute Press, 1981.

Leiner, Frederick C. *Millions for Defense: The Subscription Warships of 1798.* Annapolis: Naval Institute Press, 2000.

Lewis, Charles Lee. *The Romantic Decatur.* Philadelphia: University of Pennsylvania Press, 1937.

Long, David F. *Ready to Hazard: A Biography of Commodore William Bainbridge, 1774–1833,* Hanover, N.H.: University Press of New England, 1981.

McKee, Christopher. *Edward Preble.* Annapolis: Naval Institute Press, 1996.

————. *A Gentlemanly and Honorable Profession.* Annapolis: Naval Institute Press, 1991.

Mackenzie, Alexander Slidell. *Life of Stephen Decatur.* Boston: Charles C. Little & James Brown, 1848 (University Microfilms, Ann Arbor, Mich.).

Martin, Tyrone C. *A Most Fortunate Ship*. Chester, Conn.: Globe-Pequot Press, 1980.

Morris, Charles. *Autobiography*. Boston: A. Williams & Co., 1880.

Naval Documents Relating to the United States Wars with the Barbary Powers. Washington: 1939–1945, 7 vols.

Palmer, Michael J. *Stoddert's War: Naval Operations during the Quasi-War with France, 1798–1801*. Annapolis: Naval Institute Press, 2000 (reprint).

Proceedings of the General Court Martial Convened for the Trial of Commodore James Barron, Captain Charles Gordon, Mr. William Hook, and Captain John Hall, of the United States Ship CHESAPEAKE, in the month of January, 1808. Washington: Jacob Gideon, Jr., 1822.

Roosevelt, Theodore. *The Naval War of 1812*. Annapolis: Naval Institute Press, 1987.

Sale, Kirkpatrick. *The Fire of His Genius: Robert Fulton and the American Dream*. New York: Free Press, 2001.

Stevens, William Oliver. *An Affair of Honor: The Biography of James Barron, U.S.N.* Virginia: Norfolk County Historical Society of Chesapeake, 1969.

Tracy, Nicolas, ed. *The Naval Chronicle*, Vol. 4, 1807–1810, and vol. 5, 1811–1815. London: Stackpole Books, Chatham Publishing, 1999.

Truman, Major Ben C. *The Field of Honor: A . . . History of Duelling*. New York: Fords, Howard & Hulbert, 1884.

Tucker, Spencer T., and Reuter, Frank T. *Injured Honor: The Chesapeake–Leopard Affair June 22, 1807*. Annapolis: Naval Institute Press, 1996.

Waldo, S. Putnam. *Life and Character of Stephen Decatur* (2d ed.). Middletown, Conn.: Oliver D. Cooke, 1822.

Watson, Paul Barron. *The Tragic Career of Commodore James Barron*. New York: Coward McCann, 1942.

Whipple, A. B. C. *To the Shores of Tripoli*. New York: William Morrow and Company, 1991.

Notes and Comments

Chapter 1

My Rand McNally Road Atlas lists towns, cities, and counties named after Decatur in Alabama, Arkansas, Georgia, Illinois, Indiana, Iowa, Kansas, Michigan, Mississippi, Nebraska, Tennessee, and Texas. There are undoubtedly many other less official place names, such as Fort Decatur in Gales Ferry, Connecticut, a few miles from my home.

Chapter 2

A curious newspaper article, published a half century after Decatur's death, claimed that as an adolescent he was implicated in a murder. The Wilmington (Delaware) *Daily Commercial* of December 22, 1874, ran a story asserting that Decatur struck and killed a prostitute on the streets of Philadelphia, for which act he was arrested, tried for life, and eventually acquitted. "Stephen is said to have been in his raising quite a desperate youth," the article stated. "His father could exercise little restraining authority over him. He was self-willed, high spirited, dissipated and reckless. He was finally persuaded to enter a certain well-known mercantile house, but grew worse and worse." The uncorroborated description of Decatur as a confirmed sociopath is so out of keeping with the known facts of his life that I find it highly suspicious. Would Commodore Barry have recommended such a youth for a midshipman's warrant? Could such a wild and abandoned Decatur have earned the devotion of such a friend as the studious Richard Rush? Charles Lee Lewis, in his 1937 biography of Decatur, stated that he had "in vain attempted to verify this story." Neither he nor anyone else seems to have come up with any supporting evidence. There are, of course, numerous examples of wild youths who have settled down to lead distinguished and productive lives, but I find this story literally incredible.

Relative to Decatur's difficulties at school, it seems likely that he suffered from what today would be recognized as a learning disability, perhaps from some form of dyslexia. This mild handicap may explain the curiously spotty paper trail Decatur left behind to mark his career. Naval officers, and ship's captains in particular, must deal with a mountain of paperwork, and in the course of carrying out their duties they tend to generate voluminous records in the form of logs, letters, invoices, orders, journals, and reports, which provide invaluable information for historians. But scholars have traditionally complained that Decatur left little beyond the bare minimum required by his official duties. It may well be that the paucity of data stems from Decatur's difficulty with the written word, and could explain what he himself characterized in a letter to his brother John (August 1, 1816) as "my procrastinating disposition."

Chapter 3

The sentence about "personal honor and ship's honor" is taken almost word for word from Edward Beach's *United States Navy: 200 Years*. Captain Beach's phrasing was so succinct and eloquent that I did not wish to tamper with it.

The discussion of fame, honor, and glory is based almost entirely on an essay by Douglass Adair entitled "Fame and the Founding Fathers," from his book of the same name.

Chapter 4

The story of Richard Somers's bizarre multiple duels, which seems almost beyond belief, is undoubtedly true. It is authenticated by Charles Washington Goldsborough, editor of *The Naval Chronicle, Volume 1* (Washington: 1824), who had previously served as chief clerk of the navy. In his account of the incident, Goldsborough justified the extreme nature of the duel by pointing out "that all the parties were very *young men*" (his italics). Goldsborough does not specify the time and place of the duel. Lewis thought it occurred in 1801 in the Mediterranean, when the parties involved would all have been commissioned officers, but it seems evident to me that it must have occurred earlier than that, at a time when Decatur and Somers—and their peers—would still be midshipmen, and young enough for such foolishness.

When Decatur's brother-in-law, Marine Captain James McKnight, was killed in a duel in Italy, his commanding officer, Captain Alexander Murray of the *Constellation,* refused on moral grounds to attend the funeral, publicly charging that McKnight had died for a false idea of honor. In his report of the death to the secretary of the navy, Murray wrote, "The unhappy catastrophe of Captain McKnight, who was a very deserving officer, though rather irritable, induces me to wish that an article might be inserted in the regulations for the navy, rendering every officer liable to heavy penalties and even to loss of his commission for giving or receiving a challenge and also the seconds for aiding and abetting in such unwarrantable acts." Murray's anger makes it clear that not everyone in the navy took dueling for granted.

Chapter 5

Decatur's comment before the destruction of the *Philadelphia* is traditionally given as, "The fewer the number, the greater the honor." The source is Charles Morris's recollection of the event, which was written half a century after the action. Frederick Leiner, in an article in *Naval History* (October 2001), was the first to point out that Decatur's quotation as given by Morris closely parallels Henry V's comment to Westmoreland just before his St. Crispian's speech (Act IV, Scene 3). It seems likely to me that Decatur would have quoted Shakespeare correctly and Morris, not recognizing the source, would have remembered it with a slight inaccuracy. See also Douglass Adair's "Fame and the Founding Fathers" for the influence of Shakespeare's *Henry V* in the early republic.

Salvadore Catalano, the Sicilian pilot who played such a key role in the attack on the *Philadelphia* in Tripoli harbor, remained in the service of the American navy for the rest of his life. He received an appointment as sailing master in 1809, and died an American citizen in 1846.

Chapter 6

Was it Reuben James or Daniel Frazier? The story of the sailor who saved Decatur's life by selflessly taking the blow meant for his captain quickly became a staple of tales of the sea, and was a favorite of boys' literature for over a century, but there has long been a controversy about the identity of the man who performed the heroic act. Some claim he was a sailor named Daniel Frazier, variously spelled Fraser, or Frashier. In support of the claim, they point to the medical report of those men wounded on Decatur's boat for that day, which records,

"Dnl. Frashier, two incised wounds on the head, one of them severe; one bad wound across the wrist and seven slightly about his hands." Reuben James's name does not appear at all in the report. Certain it is that Daniel Frazier spent his declining years stoutly maintaining that he was the one who saved Decatur. On the other hand, one of the earliest authorities on Decatur, Commander Alexander Slidell Mackenzie, a naval officer who interviewed many of Decatur's friends, relatives, and associates in preparation for writing his biography of Decatur, wrote in 1848, "The writer is aware that the act ascribed to Reuben James, has been sometimes ascribed to Daniel Frazer, another favorite follower of Decatur. After examining all the testimony on the subject, and having recently conversed with officers, who had the particulars of the encounter from Reuben James himself, and who saw the deep wound in the head, which he received on the occasion, the writer is convinced that he was the real actor in this memorable scene of self-devotion." It is not likely we will ever know with absolute certainty which man deserves the credit.

Chapter 7

An incident relating to the death of Richard Somers provides an interesting insight into the overbearing self-importance and pomposity of Commodore William Bainbridge. Edward Preble, in his official dispatch touching on Somers's heroic death, praised Somers and his fellow officers for declaring that they would blow themselves up rather than be captured. Bainbridge, highly sensitive to the fact that he had surrendered the *Philadelphia* under equivocal circumstances, took personal umbrage at what he saw as an implied criticism of himself, and Preble had to write him a long soothing letter to smooth his ruffled feathers.

No one has ever identified Stephen Decatur's Philadelphia fiancée. W. M. P. Dunne believed the evidence pointed to Mary King, the granddaughter of Rufus King, the noted Federalist politician. The romance was purported to have blossomed when King and his family were in Philadelphia during his tenure as a senator from New York, which ended in 1796. This would suggest that the young couple had known each other for over ten years before Decatur broke the engagement in 1805. Dunne admitted that "firm evidence of the young lady is lacking." Unless some long-lost letters surface, it is unlikely we will ever know the young lady's identity.

Chapter 8

There is an interesting anomaly that sometimes causes confusion concerning the correct date of the *Chesapeake–Leopard* Affair. Tucker and Reuter, in their book on the incident, specify that it took place on June 22, 1807. Other authorities, including Craig L. Symonds, in his *Historical Atlas of the U.S. Navy* (Annapolis: Naval Institute Press, 1995), set the date as June 23, 1807. Both are correct. On land, the sailing navy followed the general calendar and reckoned dates from midnight to midnight, but at sea, the day was reckoned from the sun's meridian, that is, from noon to noon. The *Chesapeake* left Hampton Roads on June 22, but that afternoon, when the *Leopard* attacked, both ships were at sea, and it was therefore June 23.

Chapter 9

HMS *Leopard,* after being banished by Captain Thomas Hardy to Bermuda, remained a part of the North American Squadron but never returned to the United States. She was eventually wrecked in 1814 off the island of Anticosti, in the Gulf of St. Lawrence. The Royal Navy has commissioned at least four subsequent *Leopard*s, but in deference to American sensitivities, the Admiralty instituted standing orders prohibiting any British warship named *Leopard* from ever being sent to an American port.

The two French ships that had sought shelter in Chesapeake ports, and whose presence in America had precipitated the British blockade, escaped into the Atlantic in the autumn of 1807 when the British blockading ships temporarily abandoned the Virginia Capes so that their officers might attend Captain Hardy's wedding in Halifax.

Chapter 10

By 1812, British officials had long since disavowed the 1807 attack on the *Chesapeake,* but since they refused to accept any responsibility for the act, they had neglected to return the sailors kidnapped on the occasion. On July 10, 1812, just days after Congress had declared war, the Royal Navy decided to rectify the situation. In a last-minute effort to tidy up some unfinished business, the British schooner *Brim* entered Boston harbor under a flag of truce. On board she carried the two surviving prisoners carried off by the *Leopard* all those years before. The only English-born captive, Jenkin Ratford, had been hanged for insulting a British officer on the streets of Norfolk. William Ware, one of the three American-born prisoners, had died in captivity. On July 11, the captain of the *Brim* personally delivered the last two surviving sailors, William Martin and John Strachan, to Commodore William Bainbridge on the quarterdeck of the *Chesapeake*. Bainbridge made a brief speech of welcome to the two and sent them forward to their old stations. Then, turning to the British captain, he invited him in for lunch.

Chapter 11

The account of the battle between the *United States* and the *Macedonian* given here is limited primarily to the American perspective of events. Anyone interested in how Captain Carden and his men may have seen and reacted to the same events may want to consult my *Chronicles of the Frigate Macedonian,* pp. 48–88.

There is a bittersweet addendum to the story of Jack Creamer (the name is sometimes spelled Cramer or Kreamer), the boy who asked to be put on the rolls so he could share prize money. According to Alexander Mackenzie, in his *Life of Stephen Decatur,* Decatur "subsequently obtained for him a midshipman's warrant, and made him a sharer of his after achievements. Creamer ever proved himself most worthy of his benefactor; became an excellent seaman and officer, and, compensating by indefatigable industry for the want of early advantages, was fast adding all the science and polite culture that could grace his station, when the life, which had been spared during three engagements under Decatur, was lost by the accidental upsetting of a boat on an excursion of pleasure in a remote sea."

Chapter 12

Shortly after his capture of the *Macedonian,* Decatur received word that he had been elected to the Society of the Cincinnati, and he took great pride thereafter in prominently displaying the large, distinctive order of the Society on the left breast of his uniform. The Society was established by American and French officers at the end of the American Revolution and named in honor of George Washington, who, like the ancient Roman senator Cincinnatus, returned to private life after winning a great victory that could have earned him a throne. Decatur's father had been a founder of the Society, which was open only to veterans of the Revolution with membership passing to eldest sons. The fact that Decatur so wholeheartedly accepted the honor is something of a surprise, since most of the nation's founders, regardless of party, including John Adams, Thomas Jefferson, and Benjamin Franklin, strongly opposed the Society as undemocratic and were outspoken in their condemnation of it. Decatur, whose strongly democratic sympathies were well known, saw no conflict in his membership.

Following the arrival of the *Macedonian* in New York harbor, the city fathers proposed a gala naval ball in honor of Decatur and his officers. Decatur, concerned as always for the welfare of everyone who sailed with him, asked that a similar celebration be arranged for his crew. This second and rowdier affair, which Decatur also attended, was held shortly after the dinner for the officers.

Chapter 13

In another collaboration with Robert Fulton during the time he was blockaded in New London, Decatur contributed to the inventor's development of a huge steam-powered catamaran gunboat, which Fulton called *Demologos*, which was Greek for "voice of the people." She would be a slow and ungainly thing, but because the catamaran was powered by steam, she could venture forth on a windless day, when the blockading ships were helpless to move from their anchorages. *Demologos* would be free to take up a position where British broadsides could not reach her, and at her leisure pound the blockaders into kindling. Decatur realized that the *Demologos*, if employed off New London, could instantly free his squadron. Such a ship was in fact built in New York, but was not ready until after the war. She remains a significant milestone in naval history—the world's first steam warship—but she did nothing to alleviate Decatur's frustration.

The unfortunate Midshipman William Cox of the *Chesapeake,* who was banished from the navy as a result of the draconian judgment of Decatur's court, lived on until 1874 under the cloud of his overly harsh sentence. After his death his family mounted a campaign to clear his name, and as a result of what must have been herculean efforts over several generations, they finally managed in 1952 to get a joint resolution through Congress, supported by two successive directors of naval history, that authorized the president "to issue the late William S. Cox a commission as a third lieutenant, effective the date of his death." A hundred and thirty-nine years after the court-martial, a wrong was finally righted.

Chapter 14

Edward L. Beach has posed an intriguing question relating to the New York pilots who ran the *President* up onto the bar off Sandy Hook, causing the damage and delay that subsequently resulted in the frigate's capture. In *The United States Navy: 200 Years,* Beach asked, "With the given capabilities of the British Secret Service, is it beyond imagining that those pilots, or whoever placed the marker boats, made a less than honest mistake?"

Chapter 15

The *President* was the only American super frigate to be taken in the war, and the Royal Navy was eager to get her home and put her on display as a trophy. Captain Hope, of HMS *Endymion,* was put in charge of sailing her to England, and he encouraged people to think that it was his ship (which in fact had been left dead in the water by the *President*) that had been responsible for capturing her. The *President* was found to be in such poor condition, as a result of the damage she had sustained when grounded on the bar, that she brought in prize money only $64,789.50.

Chapter 16

Constitutional scholars are still uncertain as to the authorship of certain of the *Federalist Papers* and would undoubtedly give much to locate Stephen Decatur's copy, annotated by James Madison. My editor, Bill Rosen, put it succinctly in a note to me: "The idea of having Madison annotate Decatur's own copy of the *Federalist Papers* is like having Albert Einstein help you with your physics homework."

Decatur's "right or wrong" toast was widely acclaimed in America, but others viewed it with a certain bewildered skepticism. *Niles' Weekly Register* quoted a wry British reaction: "There seems to be a strange want of correct ideas upon almost every subject in America. Thus one of the most estimable officers in the American service, a brave and humane man, commodore Decatur, gave as a public toast lately, 'Our country: in her course with other nations, may she be always right, and always successful right or wrong.' And this toast the official paper of the American government calls, 'a just sentiment never better expressed—a noble patriotism never more beautifully illustrated.'"

Chapter 17

A chilling example of Jesse Duncan Elliott's perverse character is vividly expressed in the historical anecdote that Tyrone Martin, chronicler of the USS *Constitution,* refers to as "Elliott's pickled cat." When serving as commodore of the Mediterranean Squadron late in his career, Elliott stipulated that the ship's cat o' nine tails be preserved in brine when not in use, because the salt would increase the pain of flogging.

Chapter 18

The citation from Littleton W. Tazewell's letter, dated Norfolk, March 12, 1820, is from a copy made early in the twentieth century by William Decatur Parsons from the original in his possession. The copy is owned by Stephen Decatur, Jr., of Marblehead, Massachusetts. Mackenzie quotes from the letter in his biography of Decatur, but does not specify Tazewell as the author.

Chapter 19

The two principal eyewitness accounts of the duel are the one written on the day of the duel by Decatur's supernumerary, Samuel Hambleton, and the considerably more detailed one written by James Barron in 1842, many years after the event.

Chapter 20

According to Sarah Tapper, Curator of Collections at Decatur House, after Susan Decatur moved out of her home, she retained title to the property until 1836, when it was lost for back taxes. In 1988, the remains of Susan Decatur were removed from Georgetown and reinterred near those of her husband in St. Peter's churchyard in Philadelphia.

Index

231

About the Author

JAMES TERTIUS DE KAY is the widely praised author of a number of fast-paced, highly readable books of naval history, including *Monitor, Chronicles of the Frigate Macedonian, The Battle of Stonington,* and *The Rebel Raiders,* as well as a number of young adult histories, and books on left-handedness. He lives in Pawcatuck, Connecticut.